ODD JOBS

One Man's Life Working Every Gig He Could Find, from Bathroom Attendant to Bikini Model

Jonathan Krieger

This is a work of nonfiction. The names of people, places and businesses have often been changed. Certain pieces of dialogue may be inexact, because remembering specific conversations word-for-word is really hard. Seriously, you try it.

2018 TEN17 PRESS Paperback Edition

Copyright © 2018 by Jonathan Krieger

All rights reserved. No part of this book may be reproduced or used in any manner without written permission of the copyright owner except for the use of quotations in a book review. For more information, write to jonathan@jonathankrieger.com

If, by the time you read this, that e-mail address is no longer valid, that's really on you. Even if Jonathan has become a recluse, living in a cabin, overwhelmed by the mass of fandom clamoring for his next book, you still must find him and obtain his consent. He will act angry that you dared disturb him, but deep down, he will be happy to know you care.

First paperback edition November 2018

Cover design by Aleksandra Dabic

ISBN 978-1-7309-2248-0

www.jonathankrieger.com

1 1 2 3 5 8 13 21 34

Dedication

I didn't like Ms. Middleton at first. She was crass and loud. The kind of person you met at a bar, not in a classroom. But she loved writers, she loved her students, and she believed in me. I still remember an essay I wrote for her called, "War, What Is It Good For?" It was completely devoid of any thought or analysis, but it had the kind of poetically worded sentences teachers love. The kind that made it look like a quality, insightful piece deserving of an A, even if it wasn't one. Ms. Middleton was nice enough to tell me it was garbage, and I was better than that. We all need someone who can tell us they love our work, but give us a kick in the butt when we deserve it. I always dreamed of giving her the first book I published as a gift. The fantasy feels like a memory. I can hear her excited squeal and feel her crushing hug as I hand her an autographed copy. But I didn't get the chance. She passed away in 2006 at age 64. Teachers like her are why school matters. I hope they get new releases wherever you are, Ms. Middleton. I hope this makes you proud.

When I was a boy of fourteen, my father was so ignorant I could hardly stand to have the old man around. But when I got to be twenty-one, I was astonished at how much he had learned in seven years.

-Mark Twain

Table of Contents

Past Work Experience
Unemployment
Odd Job #1: Landmine Detector Tester
Odd Job #2: Crazy Couponer
Odd Job #3: Assistant Regional Manager
Odd Job #4: Bouncer
Two Weeks' Notice
Odd Job #5: Blood Donor
Odd Job #6: Ghost Writer
Odd Job #7: Research Study Participant
Dream Job
Odd Job #8: Panhandler
Headhunters
Odd Job #9: Afterschool Teacher
Odd Job #10: Brand Ambassador
Odd Job #11: Bikini Model
Odd Job #12: Depressed Research Study Participant
Side Hustle
Odd Job #13: Mickey Mouse
Odd Job #14: Balloon Artist
Odd Job #15: Professional Basketball Player
Odd Job #16: Bathroom Attendant
Career Change
Odd Job #17: Workout Novice
Odd Job #18: Conjoined Twin

Odd Job #19: Engineer
Odd Job #20: Bargain Hunter
The Want Ads
Odd Job #21: Game Show Applicant
Odd Job #22: Rock Star
Odd Job #23: Substitute Teacher
Odd Job #24: Writer/Entertainer

Past Work Experience

July 2010

The woman on the other end of the phone sounded like she'd smoked too many cigarettes in her life. She sounded like she'd been up until 4 a.m. the night before. And she sounded like she didn't have time for my crap. In short, she sounded like Vegas.

"Yeah honey, you missed the deadline to wire your buy-in," she told me. "You'll have to do it in person." A few weeks earlier, I had won $12,000 in an online poker tournament that, unlike your average tournament, had one special condition: The winner was supposed to use $10,000 of the prize money to buy into the World Series of Poker Main Event in Las Vegas—arguably the biggest poker competition on the planet.

I had assumed that the website that hosted the original tournament would handle the logistics of signing me up for the Main Event, but instead they had sent me the $12,000 via bank transfer and left me to do the rest. For some reason, it hadn't occurred to me that I might have trouble registering over the phone.

"So, what do I do?" I asked. "Bring $10,000 cash in my right pocket on a flight to Las Vegas?"

"Yeah, that's what I would do."

"Isn't it illegal to carry that much on a plane? Won't security stop me?"

She gave an exhausted sigh, as though she couldn't believe we were still on this. "I just wouldn't tell them about the money. What are they gonna do, check you?"

It occurred to me that since I would be at an airport, yes, they might check me.

But I clearly didn't have much of a choice. So I found myself standing in line at the bank, trying to act like I wasn't there to withdraw massive quantities of money. As I waited, I eyed the other customers, each one a potential mugger. Someone who might overhear me taking out $10,000 and decide it would be worth his time to follow me home, stick a knife in my side, and make off with the loot.

"Can I help whoever's next?" the teller called out, and I walked up to her window.

"I'd like to make a withdrawal," I said, trying to be as quiet as possible.

"A WHAT?!" the teller seemed to be shouting. I looked around at everyone who couldn't care less, convinced their ears were now tuned towards me.

"A withdrawal," I murmured.

"HOW MUCH?!" she bellowed.

"$10,000."

"$10,000?! OH, I DON'T KNOW IF WE HAVE ENOUGH HUNDREDS! LET ME CHECK."

By the time she handed me my money, I was surprised it didn't come in a bag with a giant dollar sign on it. But I didn't care. I was going to Vegas.

Riding the shuttle from the airport to the Strip, all the tourists chatted excitedly about how much they would lose. Playing poker, you forget that this is how the rest of the world views gambling: as an inevitable parting between you and your money.

In most casino games, the odds are rigged slightly against you, so that as time goes on your funds slowly disappear. But in poker, you aren't competing against the house, you're competing against other players, and the casino makes its income by withdrawing a little money from every hand you play or charging you a fee upfront to join the game. If you're good enough, you can beat everyone at such a rate that you overcome these deductions and turn a profit.

It is still a game of chance, but one that a skilled player can beat over the long haul, like investing in real estate. And so you end up staring out the window, smiling at all the people who seem to take an almost perverse joy in speculating about how much they're going to lose.

Eventually, someone noticed the quiet 24-year-old in the

back seat. "Hey, you're not here for that tournament are you?" she asked.

"Yeah," I answered.

"Wow."

The conversations stopped, and everyone's head turned. "How much does it cost?"

"About ten grand," I said, trying to act like it was nothing. Suddenly the several hundred they thought they'd dump playing blackjack that night didn't seem quite so audacious.

"Woooowwww. How much do you get if you win?"

The tournament was eight days long, with participants getting knocked out each day. Being among the final ten percent or so of players left standing—a distinction you would achieve if you made it partway through day four—would earn you almost $20,000. And, of course, the longer you lasted, the more you made. But they weren't asking what I'd get if I survived four days. They wanted to know what I would take home if I won the whole thing.

"First place gets around $8 million," I told them as the jaws dropped. Throw in a $10 million sponsorship deal that went to whoever won, and first place was worth nearly $20 million before taxes. That was, assuming you could outlast over 7,000 opponents, including most of the top players in the world.

"Oooooh... Well, don't forget us when you're rich."

It was a line I had heard a lot leading up to the Series. But what was there to remember? *Oh, you were on that bus ride to the Rio? Well then, here's five grand!*

I smiled and assured them I wouldn't. As with everyone else who told me to remember them if I won, I felt certain they would forget all about me if I lost.

The competition kicked off the next day and I, a historically poor sleeper, couldn't sleep. I woke up around 3 a.m., wasted an hour and a half trying to doze back off, then gave up and headed downstairs from my room.

The floors were still littered with stray gamblers on late-night benders pouring money into slot machines and unloading their wallets at the craps tables.

I walked to the tournament room and looked out on a sea of empty tables and chairs. Strolling through it all, I felt like a rookie called up to the majors, stepping onto the field in an empty stadium the morning of his first game. Soon, this place would be filled with shuffling chips and the juice of millions of dollars on the line. Soon, there would be cameras from ESPN and poker superstars filling the floor. But right now, it was only me and a few janitors. Silent.

The hours ticked by like days, slowly grinding toward lunch time. In return for my $10,000 buy-in, the Rio had given me a $10 food voucher for the nearby cafeteria. So, you know, not a bad deal. I had told myself I would eat healthy during my trip to help maintain stamina, and this was my first real meal since making that pledge.

"Chicken fingers and fries with a Pepsi," I told the man behind the counter. This was about how long most of my healthy eating resolutions lasted.

"Are you playing today?" I heard someone behind me ask as I waited.

I turned around to find a tiny old woman staring up at me

with starry eyes, her husband standing beside her.

"Yeah," I answered. "You?"

"Oh, no. Just here to watch. Our nephew always dreamed of playing. But he died three months ago. So now you get to live his dream."

I stared at her, dumbstruck. What do you say to that? *Well... have fun watching!*

"I guess so," I said, then headed for my table.

Talking to people before leaving home, I had acted humble. "We'll see what happens," I told them. "I'm sure I'm making a giant mistake not just keeping the money." Like I said, I was supposed to use what I had won to buy into the World Series, but once the website had deposited the money in my bank account, it was mine. I could have just decided to keep it. Instead I had let it ride on a $10,000 gamble.

But, internally, I wasn't worried. It was almost like I knew I was going to win. Maybe not the $8 million, but at least $20,000. After all, I was better than almost everyone I normally played against. My friends. People at casinos. The competition in the low-stakes online poker rooms. Why should this be any different? I was going to take a wrecking ball to this freakin' thing.

Or so I thought.

It was about ten hands into play that I realized just how outgunned I was. The guy on my left saw through my every move. He called when I bluffed and folded when I was strong. The guy to his left was fearless. As the game went along, friends of his kept coming over to give him a hard time about the tens of thousands of dollars he had lost betting on soccer games over the last few days or to joke about the $80,000 hand they had played the night before. This buy-in meant nothing to him, and not caring if you lose is power. He bullied all of us and steamrolled over me like I was nothing. Which, I suppose, I was.

I started to get in my head, started thinking about all the more financially prudent things I could have done with the $10,000. Man did I wish I hadn't committed to posting updates to Facebook about how I was doing.

"1,700," came my opponent's bet.

Your buy-in gets you 30,000 in chips. Once those are gone, you're eliminated. And I was down to my last 12,000. Meanwhile, my hand was terrible. I needed a nine to catch a straight, or else I was dead. If I called, I was betting almost 15 percent of my chips for a pot I had about an eight percent chance of winning.

"I call." I heard the words coming out of my mouth like someone else had spoken them. The right play was to fold. My brain was screaming "fold." But I wasn't acting logically anymore. If you take enough hits over the course of a game, you stop making the plays you think will work and start making the ones you hope will work. And anytime you're hoping in poker, you're in trouble.

Then came the next card.

Nine of hearts.

As card players like to say, it's better to be lucky than good.

That's when things turned. I caught a run of quality hands. I won a huge pot off the big bad bully, and suddenly he wasn't so intimidating anymore. The player to my left, who had such a strong read on me, had won so much that he now seemed content to simply fold the rest of his hands and advance to the next day. I picked up a pair of kings. Then ace-king. Then aces. As my confidence returned and my opponents began to fear me, I bluffed more, stealing pots and stacking chips.

I finished the day with 88,000 chips, good for a spot in the top five percent of everyone competing.

Day two was more of the same. I came out strong, climbing over 100,000. And all I could think about was how much money I was going to make. About how I was going to come back home as the guy who took on Vegas and won. You'd think I would have learned my lesson about getting cocky from the day before.

There's a line in the film *Rounders*—a Matt Damon poker movie that is virtually required watching for anyone in a card room—where Damon, quoting a poker book, says, "Few players recall big pots they have won, strange as it seems, but every player can remember with remarkable accuracy the outstanding tough beats of his career." And that about sums it up. Because it's been five years, and I can still remember every detail of what happened, right down to the suit of each player's cards.

They call them bad beat stories. Players experience a cruel twist of fate, and they want to tell everyone who will listen, which is unfortunate since no one else cares. You got unlucky in a game of chance? That's crazy!

But I can queue those memories up and play them in my brain like I'm watching scenes from a video. My opponents caught flushes on back-to-back hands, including one I never saw coming. As I watched them scooping up giant pots full of my chips, my brain started to feel like a misfiring computer. It didn't fully understand what had happened, only that something had gone very wrong.

An hour into play the next day, I was out of chips. Just another tourist who took his shot and lost. As I headed for the exits, I told myself that making it to day three wasn't bad for my first time in the World Series, and I'd be back again soon.

I was wrong.

Unemployment

August 2010-April 2011

The World Series was just supposed to be a fun vacation. The plan was that when it was all over, I would fly home and go back to my regular job working 40 hours a week and collecting a paycheck. Though hopefully I would do it with an extra 20 grand in my bank account.

But by the time I returned, something had changed. Before Vegas, professional poker players had always seemed like mythical figures when I watched them on TV. Number-crunching, mind-reading savants doing something most mortals couldn't. But competing in that tournament, I was struck by how ordinary so many of the people making a living in this field seemed. If they could do it, why couldn't I?

The internet was full of resources for aspiring card sharks looking to take their skills to the next level: podcasts and blogs offering advice, forums debating proper strategy, YouTube videos of the game's elite. These had always been things I consumed in an effort to improve, but now I devoured them. Any time I was stuck in traffic or cooking meals, I was rethinking past hands, dissecting what I could have done differently. And when I wasn't working or studying, I was playing.

In November of 2010, four months after my World Series washout, online poker became my exclusive source of income. I wasn't rich, but I made enough to support myself and pay the bills, and that was plenty. I would get up, spend my mornings and afternoons submerged in my favorite game, then hang out with friends at night. Even better, I achieved the American Dream: I got to spend my entire workday in pajamas.

Unfortunately, all pants-free adventures must come to an end.

In the gambling community, it's called "Black Friday." April 15, 2011 was the day the Justice Department shut down the major online poker companies operating in America. At the time, I was visiting a friend in Chicago. After she went into work for the day, I opened my laptop to log onto a website called FullThrottle,[1] where I normally played. But instead of seeing the usual array of poker tables I could hop in and join, I saw a webpage with the seals of the Department of Justice and the Federal Bureau of Investigation. Below those were words that

---

[1] The names of companies, people, and locations in this book have been changed. If you have your guesses about which site I actually played on based on this pseudonym, well, who's to say if you're right or wrong?

read like a foreclosure sign on a house. They explained that the domain had been seized by the FBI as part of an arrest warrant from the US Attorney's Office and then proceeded to spell out multiple crimes FullThrottle stood accused of.

That was it. There were no links or options to go elsewhere. A place where millions of global dollars flowed daily had been replaced by one page listing daunting charges brought by the people who catch criminals.

The gist of those charges was that the online poker companies, and the banks who transferred players' money to them, had broken a number of laws, and as such their assets were now in jeopardy of being seized. Assets which included the thousands of dollars I had won over the last few months that were currently resting in FullThrottle's accounts, along with the money of legions of players just like me.

When I had told people how I was making my living over the previous few months, many reacted as though I had said I was dealing weed out of my apartment. "Isn't that illegal?" they would ask in a voice that was simultaneously excited and concerned.

I would assure them that playing online poker was completely legit. Technically, the companies operating these gambling hubs were violating US law, but since they were all based overseas that didn't matter.

But I had missed something.

Several years earlier, the SAFE Port Act of 2006, a bill increasing funding to fight terrorism, had become law. It was the kind of we-all-agree-that-terrorism-is-bad, right? legislation that came up every now and then and passed with no debate and near-unanimous approval. It also included an unrelated rider many never even noticed called the Unlawful Internet Gambling Enforcement Act (or UIGEA) that made it illegal for online gambling establishments to process US citizens' funds and, more importantly, for financial institutions to transfer US citizens' funds to those gambling establishments.

The DOJ had evidence that, in an attempt to evade these laws, the poker companies had bribed failing banks to process payments they shouldn't have and misrepresented themselves to other financial entities so people could still deposit money online.[2]

Unfortunately, whether or not I had done anything illegal was only part of the story. Since almost all my money was stored in the accounts of a business whose assets were frozen, not only had I lost my only source of income, I was also broke.

When I opened up the FullThrottle site that day, my world instantly went numb. At dinner with my friends that night, it felt like they were a television set on low volume in the background. As they chatted away, all I could think about was how royally screwed I was.

To make matters worse, I owed taxes on my winnings despite the fact that they were effectively gone. On April 14, I was a professional poker player, making a living doing something I enjoyed with money to spare. On April 16, I was

---

[2] When I initially put $100 into an online poker account, the transaction showed up on my checking account statement as going to a golf supplies store. I thought it was weird, but figured maybe that was the name of a parent company or something and went on with my life. It turned out online poker sites were using fake business names when accepting player funds so financial institutions either wouldn't know their customers were sending money to an online gambling entity or, at the very least, had plausible deniability. It was countless acts of alleged fraud like this one that had inspired the DOJ to take action.

broke, unemployed, and in debt.

And you thought you hated April 15.

For the next few days, any time people wanted to discuss anything other than my plight, I barely listened. Of course, if they ever did want to talk about it, it was mostly to tell me that things would be okay, which only made me want to change the subject because they clearly didn't get it.

I remember sitting in my parents' living room as my father was telling me about the time he got fired. About how he had been a successful scientist earning a good paycheck until a new chairman took over and decided the department needed restructuring, leaving him unemployed.

As he spoke, I reflected on that period from my childhood. Back then, inside my 10-year-old bubble, I hadn't noticed much of what my family was going through, save for the fact that we seemed to go out for dinner less often. What I didn't see were my parents' discussions about how they could afford to keep my sister in college or whether to sell the house.

My father ended up working several different jobs in the ensuing years, each inducing its own set of struggles, as he tried to support the family. But, ultimately, he found the perfect fit. He started his own business doing grant consulting for biotech companies, helping them get funding. Every project was an opportunity to learn about a new field of science and assist an institution that was trying to change the world. In addition, there was an excitement and freedom that came from being an entrepreneur. He gave people good jobs and was once again able to provide for us.

As we sat there in the living room, he explained how he would never have gotten to where he was if he hadn't a) been laid off and b) learned sales at his subsequent jobs. In fact, he went on, what right then seemed devastating to me could some day seem a blessing, just as it had for him.

He then quoted that age-old line, "When life gives you lemons, make lemonade."

As he spoke, I contemplated a simple thought that often comes to me in times of struggle: My father has no idea what the hell he is talking about.

My new adjectives reverberated in my head. Broke. Unemployed. In debt.

So I hopped on Craigslist to search for work. Even that action was demoralizing. Just a few months earlier, I had excitedly told myself that my new career as a professional gambler ensured that this was something I would never do again. Now here I was, scanning an array of crummy possibilities so I could make rent.

I crossed out potential options in my mind. *Can't do that. Need experience for that. Eight dollars an hour for that?!*

However, as I waded through the listings, I noticed some that weren't exactly jobs. They were more like gigs. Random things to earn money that you never saw at career fair booths. One post advertised a website called rentafriend.com where someone could lease your friendship for $10 an hour. Of course, you had to weigh those potential earnings against the ransom money your loved ones would have to spend once they inevitably started receiving pieces of your ear in the mail, but still... ten bucks an hour!

Then there was the ad titled, "Adult film studio seeking models," because if there's one place where you want to respond to a notice placed by an adult film studio, it's Craigslist. Others offered thousands if you were willing to stay in a windowless room for a couple of weeks as part of a sleep study, which, next to rentafriend and the adult film studio options, sounded delightful.

For all the creepiness, there was also something intriguing about these. They represented unique experiences rather than the repetitiveness of traditional work. Plus, they seemed like they might make for some good stories. And in that, there was opportunity.

For most of my life, I had wanted to be a writer. Since the moment in elementary school when our teacher gave us 30 minutes and told us we could write whatever we wanted, that feeling of putting words to the page to tell a story—there was something about it that left my brain swimming in a perfect cocktail of excitement and contentment.

Of course, this didn't mean I had actually done a whole lot of writing. Rather, I knew I loved it, told people it was what I wanted to do, and then barely ever did it. (This is, by the way, the action plan for 90 percent of all people who want to be writers.)

It's like the way we all know we feel better when we exercise and eat healthy, and yet so many of our attempts to do exactly that end with us watching Netflix, ordering takeout, and saying we'll try again tomorrow. Sometimes the things that will make you the happiest are the hardest to do, and it's not at all clear why.

So as I scanned the want ads of the bizarre, I decided that this was my chance to start writing again.

A couple of months after my online poker career went bust, I launched *Odd Jobs*, a blog where each entry was about something different I did to earn money. Over the next few years, I serenaded a guy with a One Direction song on Valentine's Day, begged for spare change in downtown Boston, and delivered a copy of the *Sports Illustrated* swimsuit issue while dressed in a bikini.

A few entries in, the premise of the blog broadened to include any attempt I made to improve my financial situation, even if it was unsuccessful. So I wrote about becoming a crazy couponer, flunking my gameshow audition, and losing $70 making balloon animals.

When I still wasn't earning enough to make ends meet, I picked up longer-term employment that I chronicled as well. Like my several-month stint as a manager at a fraudulent market research company and my multi-year career as a superhero at kids' birthday parties.

And as those experiences impacted me in ways I hadn't expected, I wrote about that, too.

I performed over 50 "odd jobs" as I strived to fill out my income and keep my head above water. In the process, these gigs did more than just help me survive; they slowly reshaped my world. This book is a collection of my favorite blog posts and the story of my life during that time.

Black Friday was the day my poker career ended. This is what happened next.

The things you are about to read are all real stories about real events that actually happened. No seriously, they are.

In most cases, though, the names and identifying details of the people, businesses, and locations discussed have been altered. I have included my favorite entries from my Odd Jobs *blog as well as a few never before posted online. They have been polished, as putting together a book leaves more opportunity for revision than does posting something to a website once a week. However, I strived to make sure that this editing in no way affected my portrayal of the emotions and thoughts I was experiencing at the time I wrote them. In some cases, present-day comments have been added in the form of footnotes.*

In between the blog posts are entries detailing what was happening in my life at the time. These sections (which you will be able to differentiate by the fact that they don't have the words "Odd Job" in the title and that they are preceded by the month and year they happened) were written in 2016, after I had concluded the blog and was looking back on my experiences from the previous five years.

Odd Job #1: Landmine Detector Tester

How I found the gig: Craigslist

Time worked: 1.5 hours

Pay: $30

In the movies, the soldiers were always men, they were always rugged, and they were always the kind of guys who would have stuffed people like us into our lockers in high school.

We were not real soldiers. We were the three people who showed up for Harvard University's research study testing new military technology. The frail 5'2" girl; the guy I saw reading a *People* magazine article about the royal wedding in the waiting room; and me, the blogger who loved Katy Perry music.

"Today, we'll be using some new landmine-detection training technology," explained a gruff-looking military man named Jack, who was exactly the kind of made-for-cinema soldier I was talking about. He held what appeared to be a metal detector in his right hand as we all stood in a giant gymnasium with sandboxes set up behind us to represent...

Afghanistan, I guess? I'm not sure.

"Here's how these work."

He hopped into the closest box, then began moving forward, combing the detector over every inch of sand and making sure to check any patch in front of him before progressing, the machine beeping steadily. When the beeping became louder and distorted, it indicated a nearby landmine. Sweeping in from different angles and seeing where the noise intensified, he was able to determine the location of the explosive.

"So, it's probably... right..." he paused for dramatic effect, glancing at us with the cockiness of a man who not only did this for a living but also had been the one to place the landmines that morning, "here!" Then he plunged his hand into the sand and triumphantly ripped out a small, metal cylinder representing a landmine.

I assumed this was not the military-approved removal technique.

"You'll do four ten-minute practice runs where you'll have to locate every mine and its center amidst ten yards of sand. Now I'll warn you: Your first run will be an abortion. That's fine. Don't worry about it. We'll critique your performance and, for some of you, we'll give feedback using our new technology. Once you've finished the practice rounds, you'll do a final, 15-minute, 25-yard test, and we'll see if the training helped."

The three of us glanced at each other, all obviously thinking the same thing: *Did he just say "abortion"?*

I stepped into the first sandbox, and it felt surprisingly real. There I was, traversing the desert, scanning for deadly explosives while my drill sergeant used crass language in the background. When the beeping grew louder, I became tense and focused. When it subsided, I relaxed.

Those noises were the sound of safety as I wandered through danger. When I finished, Jack came over to check my results.

"Nice," he declared. "Three for three."

I felt a surge of pride as though I had successfully identified three real landmines and was receiving praise from my actual commanding officer. Then he pulled out an iPad that depicted the sweeps I made with a red line. This was the new technology.

"Now, your sweeps should be smooth lines."

My lines looked like they were drawn by a toddler with hand tremors. I felt the pride subsiding.

"Yours aren't perfect. But you still got all three."

I glanced at my fellow volunteers, who were all struggling. I thought about how they would be missing limbs or strewn out dead if these were real minefields, while I remained completely unscathed. It felt great.

Unfortunately, my initial success was hard to maintain. As we continued with our practice sessions, the noise of the detectors beeping in the background started to blend with the sounds of my machine to the point where I couldn't tell what I was hearing. I identified mines that weren't there and missed others outright. By the fourth run, Jack had to wrestle the machine from my hands as he shouted, "Here! Let me show you!"

The frustration was mounting and the beeping was giving me a headache. I felt like a real soldier. Becoming fatigued and going crazy. Hating my drill sergeant, yet desperately wanting his approval. And resenting the girl who was kicking my butt. What were they doing letting a woman into the fake military anyway?

Considering that my entire psyche had been destroyed in

45 minutes of playing in a sandbox, I felt certain I was not cut out for combat.

With my confidence shot, my ears ringing, and my frustration peaking, it was time for the final run.

It did not go well.

As Jack reviewed my work, I could feel the disgust radiating off his body. Clearly, somewhere along the way, the lines between practice and reality had blurred a bit for him, too, and we had transitioned from being study volunteers to recruits who needed to be whipped into shape. He looked at me like he was smelling a rotten fish and told me I failed.

Dejected, I slouched over to the office to pick up the $30 check for my time. The student handling the paperwork looked at my results and gave me a conciliatory, "It can be really hard for some people."

I wondered if he had participated in the study as well. Because in his voice, I detected a level of compassion that made me think he had struggled with the technology, too.

So I guess the test proved what we already knew: Harvard students and bloggers are meant to chronicle the study, while people a lot manlier than us belong on the landmine-filled battlefields. Ya know, people like husky drill sergeants, frail 5'2" girls and guys who read *People* magazine articles about the royal wedding.

Odd Job #2: Crazy Couponer

How I found the gig: Read an article about the concept

Time worked: Unknown

Pay: A cornucopia of stuff

For years I had been going to CVS, waiting half an hour for a receipt slightly longer than a Chekhov play to print, and then throwing my proof of purchase in the trash without a second thought.

For years, I had been a fool.

This epiphany came to me while reading an article by a woman calling herself a "crazy couponer," which is, apparently, a vocation in 21st century America. She spoke of how she used coupons, rewards dollars and a bit of shamelessness to get massive quantities of stuff for free or, at least, for dramatically reduced prices.

She explained how companies offering deals to lure consumers sometimes got so carried away that they accidentally left a pathway to steep discounts that you could exploit if you knew where to look (which she of course helped you with on her blog). I had her website up seconds after finishing the newspaper story, and within a few clicks, I had made the decision that I, too, would become a crazy couponer.

I started by leafing through one of those circulars CVS keeps at the front of the store, detailing the sales they are running. I saw an ad on the last page explaining that if you bought a Hershey's Air candy bar for $0.99, you would get back $0.99 in rewards bucks. It was like getting chocolate for free! I was so excited that I didn't even bother asking the obvious question: What the hell is a Hershey's Air?

A week later, I saw they were offering free tampons,[3] so I made a beeline for the women's hygiene aisle, thereby becoming the first-ever non-sexual-predator male to walk with excited purpose to the tampon section. So what if I was going on two-and-a-half decades without menstruating?

I soon discovered that CVS wasn't the only store doing this. I nabbed a diabetes heart monitoring kit at Walgreens and scored some cough drops, hand sanitizer, lip balm, and hemorrhoid wipes at Rite Aid. All for free.

And it got better. I know what you're thinking: You can't get anything better than free hemorrhoid wipes! But you can. I found an online coupon offering $2 back if I purchased the wipes, meaning Rite Aid was paying me to buy them! With rewards bucks, a coupon, and one of my two

---

[3] For the purposes of this piece, all items that cost money but netted the same amount in rewards dollars are referred to as "free." You may say to yourself, "Well, if you bought $14 worth of stuff and then got $14 worth of rewards, you're still out $14," but you'd be wrong. Crazy couponers use a method called "ignoring seething death stares from cashiers" wherein they do multiple transactions during their visit. So if you buy seven things that each cost $2 and each yield $2 in rewards, you would buy the first one, then use the rewards on the receipt from that one to buy the next one, then use that for the next one until eventually you had all seven items plus a slip worth $2 in still-remaining rewards bucks for just the price of that initial purchase.

hemorrhoid dollars, I got a tube of toothpaste and a fancy new toothbrush to replace my horribly fraying one.

It was an exhilarating rush walking out the door with all those goodies. Though I figured I should probably find someone I could give the tampons to. Or have my period.

My roommate's girlfriend had the unfortunate fate of being the first female I saw after my shopping spree.

"Hey, random question," I said to her. Indeed, you could not get much more random than the question I was about to ask. "You want a box of tampons?"

She looked back at me, trying and failing to conceal her discomfort. "Umm... Why do you have tampons?"[4]

"It turns out CVS is practically giving away tampons," I told her, a little too excitedly. "I felt like I couldn't pass them up. But now I have them, and I don't need them."

As a rule, I hate wasting things. Though perhaps I should have made an exception.

"I guess I can take them." She seemed to be slowly realizing that if she said yes, this conversation would be over.

"Well, don't feel compelled to. I mean, would you use them? Or are you just trying to help me feel like I didn't waste my time?"

"Ummm..." At this point, my roommate walked into the room, and the conversation thankfully shifted to a different topic. She quietly took the tampons, and I don't think I looked her in the eye ever again.

I decided not to ask if she needed any hemorrhoid wipes.

---

[4] It could have been worse. She could have been completely unsurprised that I had them.

Odd Job #3:
Assistant Regional Manager

How I found the gig: Re-hired by my old boss, whom I originally met when we worked together somewhere else

Time worked: 40 hours per week

Pay: $600 per week

"Yo, Jay-Kriegs!" That was what my new boss Rick called me. "I need you to put together a letter of recommendation for Lewis."

In an attempt to add some stability to my income, I had recently taken on a more traditional job as the Assistant Regional Manager at a company called AllProfile. It was an organization with a lot of problems, and Lewis was definitely one of them.

He had a habit of showing up late, his half-hour lunch breaks frequently lasted over 90 minutes, and I had a sneaking suspicion he was spending large chunks of his shift sleeping with his eyes open. I wasn't sure he wanted anybody reading my evaluation of his workplace performance.

(It's worth noting that, despite his flaws, Lewis was arguably our best employee. He trumped Sara, who spent most of her time complaining that she didn't want to be there; Damien, who showed up exactly 20 minutes late every day due to "crazy traffic"; Ethan, who was afraid to talk to people; and Flynn, whom we hired three minutes into his interview since he was so overqualified that we felt comfortable ignoring the fact that he was clearly stoned.)

"You looking to go somewhere else?" I asked Lewis.

"Nah. I'm on trial," he answered. "The letter's for my judge."

Wait, what?

Telling me that one of our employees was a criminal must have slipped Rick's mind when he hired me. I was quickly discovering a lot of things that must have slipped Rick's mind when he hired me.

"What are you on trial for?" I asked.

I'm not sure if, legally speaking, this was something I was allowed to ask my employee. But Lewis had brought it up, and it seemed kind of relevant. If nothing else, he was a large man. And if he was going to prison for, say, aggravated assault, maybe I would stop being so hard on him about his shirt being untucked.

"I can't tell you," he answered, as he stared guiltily at his shoes. Lewis had figured out an answer even more frightening than aggravated assault.

"Well, umm… did you do it?"

"Yeah."[5]

"But if you get a good letter of recommendation, you won't go to prison?" I felt like there was a hitch somewhere in the US justice system that I wasn't understanding.

"Oh, no. I'm going to prison. It's just a matter of how long."

---

[5] Still our best employee.

I should not have taken this job.

"Come work for me," Rick had said a month earlier in that way he had of half encouraging, half pleading. We were sitting on the patio at Joey's, a restaurant where we both used to wait tables. This was the second time Rick had offered me a role as a manager at AllProfile. The first time was two years prior when I hurt my back and couldn't be a waiter anymore. That time, I had taken the position, then lasted all of three months before the dreadfulness of working there forced me to quit. Then, like now, I was broke.

AllProfile ran mall kiosks where the staff interviewed passersby about upcoming movie releases. Our employer then sold the data from those interviews to major market research companies. The problem was that there weren't a lot of mall patrons eager to take our boring, unpaid, 15-minute surveys. Almost everyone we approached would recoil and yell at us to leave them alone like we were lepers or, worse, volunteers soliciting donations for Greenpeace.

But we had a quota to fulfill, whether people took our surveys or not. Which meant that if we couldn't get enough respondents, upper management expected us to fabricate interviews. To complicate matters, AllProfile's clients knew we were instructed to falsify data, so they contracted another company to investigate and authenticate what we submitted. Roughly half of my training was spent teaching me how to create fake surveys that would pass the verification process.

Knowing how miserable I was the last time I was there, Rick assured me, "It'll be different this time. You'll be the Assistant Regional Manager. Once we get things up and running, the guys at the depots will do all the surveys while we stay home on the couch. You can spend your whole day writing if you want."

Rick himself showed up at the company kiosks less than 20 hours a week, the rest of the time leaving his employees in charge. And his offer of a chance for me to do the same was pretty appealing. More than anything, I wanted a way to pay the bills that would give me the free time to pursue the things I actually cared about. Besides, it wasn't like I had something better to fall back on.

After a couple of days spent mulling it over, I decided I could stand hating my job if it let me live the life I wanted when I wasn't on the clock. I called him up and informed him, "I would love to be your Assistant Regional Manager."

"Well, Assistant *to* the Regional Manager," he said, referencing a joke from *The Office,* a TV show we both loved. I laughed. This would be fun, I told myself.

About an hour into my first day, it was clear that Rick's sales pitch about a place that would run on autopilot was fiction. Left without proper supervision, these employees likely would have spent their shifts napping on the mattresses at the Bed World next to our kiosk. In fact, the reason Rick was able to spend so little of his time at his job was that he had people like me there cracking the whip.

And the terminable offense for Albert, the manager I was now replacing, was that he wasn't pushing his employees hard enough. They were consistently posting low numbers, which meant Rick had to come in and actually work.

During the week Albert spent training me before he was let go,[6] he told me that when people applied, he automatically hired them. He figured if they could show up to their first shift on time and in uniform, they'd be a good fit. Which, combined with our minimum-wage pay rate, certainly explained how he assembled such a Grade A squad.

For breaks, we were given 30 minutes for lunch and allowed to step away to use the bathroom or smoke a cigarette (the latter policy I'm sure only existed because Rick himself was a smoker). I made sure to visit the bathroom twice a day, regardless of whether I had to go. But I needed more time away from my station, so I started smoking.

It was gross and made me cough, and I knew how catastrophically stupid it was. But in addition to giving me an excuse not to be working, smoking gave me a chance to get some fresh air and think about how soon it would be quitting time. And so, a few hits to my long-term health seemed worth it.

"Excuse me, are you the manager of this location?" a guy in a Red Sox cap asked me.

"Yes," I answered.

"My name is Kevin, and I'm a secret shopper with ViewerTrac."

---

[6] Yup, AllProfile asked him to train me with the intention of firing him once the process was over. This was the kind of company I was working for.

ViewerTrac was one of those companies we sold our research data to. And AllProfile had assured ViewerTrac that if secret shoppers ever caught any employees falsifying surveys, those staffers would be suspended, and, if it ever happened again, they would be fired outright. This was, like most things AllProfile said, a lie. When I trained with Albert, I noticed he would always log into the computers as Arnold Sturgis. Apparently, Albert had been caught making up data, so AllProfile told the studios they were suspending him. In reality, our company simply instructed him to log into the system under a pseudonym.

But even though they protected you, AllProfile would rather you didn't get caught in the first place. If you did, you better believe you were going to hear about it. And I had a feeling this was about to be a conversation I would be hearing about.

"Nice to meet you, Kevin," I said, shaking his hand and hoping he wasn't about to say what I knew he was about to say.

"I've been watching your depot throughout the day, and I notice a lot of your employees have been completing the surveys themselves instead of having mall patrons fill them out."

My heart sank.

"I assume you know this is in direct violation of your contract with ViewerTrac?" he asked.

"Yes, I do."

"All right, well, I'm sorry, but I'm going to have to report you."

"I understand."

At this point, Damien burst out laughing.

"I'm sorry, I couldn't hold it in any longer," he said from behind me.

A smile spread across the lips of the guy in the baseball cap.

"Sorry buddy, we were busting your balls," he explained. "I'm just Damien's neighbor, I do security over there." He pointed at a pharmacy storefront behind me.

I smiled and shook his hand.

"Good one," I told him. "I really thought you were with ViewerTrac." And I kind of wished he was.

During that conversation, I reflexively felt fear over losing my job, since that's how you're supposed to react when you think you might get fired. But I also felt relief. Excitement, even, at the possibility of being able to tell Rick, "Hey man, if it were up to me, I would stay here, but after that incident with the secret shopper, what can I do?" But I couldn't. It was just a joke, and I still had my job.

The day was winding down on another long shift, and Lewis and I were the only ones left. He had shown up three hours late, and I had spent the morning leaving voicemail after voicemail on his phone demanding to know where he was. I sent text messages that yielded the response, "Be there soon. Need to help a friend with a thing." Not exactly what you wanted to hear from someone on trial for a crime he wouldn't name.

When he finally arrived, I had pulled him aside and torn into him. And as I'd shouted, I had felt my spirit leaving my body. This wasn't me. I wasn't a person who yelled at people. The place was poisoning me. I was angry all the time. Lewis just happened to be my outlet for the day.

I finished my rant. The hours passed. I cooled off. Soon we were the last two employees on an otherwise dead night.

"How are things with the trial?" I asked.

"I'm going to prison," he told me.

"Oh my God. I'm so sorry."

"Eh, it's okay. I've been there before. It's like summer camp."

"Did you just say prison is like summer camp?"

"Yeah, it's not so bad. I'll be out in a couple of years." Clearly, Lewis and I were working with different definitions of the phrase "not so bad."

"When do you go?"

"Tomorrow."

Tomorrow?? You're spending your last day as a free man logging a shift at AllProfile? I thought. *Also, how does prison work? They sentence you, and then you just sort of hang out for a few days? This is not how they do it on* Law & Order.

I wished him luck. We shook hands, and I left. He was the closing manager that day and was supposed to stay two more hours. I would later check the time clock logs and see that he left 40 minutes after I did.[7]

Can't say I blamed him. Who would stay at this place any longer than they had to

---

[7] Still our best employee.

Odd Job #4: Bouncer

How I found the gig: Hired by a friend

Time worked: 6 hours

Pay: $48

"Gene picked a hell of a night for you to train," Shorty grumbled, gazing out the window at the sleet raining down. He sighed as he turned to me. "Grab some coffee. It's gonna be a long shift."

Most people had had the same reaction when I told them that my friend Tyler had hired me to be a bouncer: poorly contained laughter. Which is fair, I suppose. I am stunningly weak for someone 6'2" and 195 pounds, the only fight I've ever been in was when I got knocked out by a single punch in second grade at a Jewish day school, and I have trouble staying awake past 11 o'clock. But still, it would have been nice if people waited to snicker until I left the room.

Unlike me, Shorty came out of the womb ready to work a nightclub door. He was a mammoth of a man, and his eyes made it clear that you wouldn't like him when he was angry. He even had the ironic nickname.

"This is your basic ID scanner," he said, holding up what looked like a credit card machine. "Stick the license in here, and it'll tell you if the card is real and whether or not the person is legal. Think you can handle that?"

"Yeah," I replied. Considering that his instructions were essentially, "Stick the card here, it'll do the rest," I felt confident in my abilities.

"Come here." He motioned his head sideways. "What do you think of Asian chicks?"

Huh?

"They're great?" I answered. *I thought we were talking about scanning IDs.*

"Check out that fine bitch at the bar."

Check out that fine bitch at the bar? Who talks like that?

There was no doubt about it, Shorty was more bouncer than I would ever be.

He took me outside, where I saw that the awning we would be stationed under was useless. The sleet was pouring in sideways, and there was a large gap in the canvas. I'd be drenched within minutes.

"This thing cost $800," Shorty said, pointing to the scanner. "Don't get it wet."

Don't get it wet? Unless this thing's got a built-in umbrella you didn't mention, it's going to get wet.

"No problem."

He looked at me like I was already screwing up, which I took as the cue to wipe off the scanner with the sleeve of my hoodie. He nodded as though I had passed some test.

When the customers finally showed up, I smiled, cracked jokes, and told everyone to have a good night as they entered. From the way Shorty eyed me, I could tell I was being too nice.

I watched as Shorty demonstrated the Tao of bouncer-dom. His gaze said he didn't trust you, and his mouth didn't say much of anything. When you walked up to him, he would grunt, "ID," then stick out his hand in a way that said you were already taking too long.

If your license checked out, he would nod his head to the door, which meant, "Yeah, sure, you can go in, now get out of my face." Unless, of course, you were hot and female. In which case, Shorty was suddenly the most welcoming maître d' you'd ever met.

Despite our different approaches, he slowly warmed to me.

"You're doing good, man," Shorty told me a few hours in. "But here's what I wanna know." His voice got lower, and he moved his face closer to mine. "If shit goes down, have you got my back?" *What? Is shit going to go down? What kind of shit? I thought we were manning the door at a bar, not robbing a bank.*

"Yeah, man," I said with all the confidence the guy who got beat up at Jew school could muster. I meant it. If something happened, I would stay and navigate the descending feces along with him. Though it was worth noting that if Shorty couldn't handle the problem, I was unlikely to be of much help.

He looked unconvinced. Like this was the Old West, and I might still prove myself yellow. "All right."

I spent the rest of the night on edge, ready for something big to happen. But it never did. There was the time I had to physically pick up an overserved patron and walk him off the patio. But the process was eased by the fact that he probably weighed 95 pounds and was too intoxicated to move his limbs.[8]

And there was the time when I admitted a girl who Shorty had to grab by the arm, yank back, and thrust in my face while shouting the words, "Really? You think she looks 21??"

I thought she did, indeed, look 21, and the scanner said her ID checked out. But I had a hunch that telling all this to Shorty would have been a mistake. So I acted mortified that I had let her through and redirected her to the 18+ entrance.

Other than that, things went smoothly, and the terrible weather turned out to be a positive. Apparently, on most nights, people were lined up for miles waiting to get in, but it was so crummy out that much of the regular clientele had stayed home.

Closing time came and went, and I helped the people inside clean up. As I trekked back and forth from the basement to the side door, carrying out a never-ending stream of trash bags, Shorty pulled me aside. "Good job tonight," he said. "Any time you wanna work with me, I'd be happy to have you."

I smiled and thanked him. I wouldn't be coming back. This was a one-time thing. A favor from a guy I played cards with who also ran the club and knew I was looking for gigs to write about. But it was still nice to hear. Coming from Shorty, it meant a lot.

It meant I was a bouncer.

---

[8] So to everyone who said I wasn't cut out to be a bouncer, let the record show that if someone is wasted and built like a stick figure, I can overpower him. Suck it.

Two Weeks' Notice

September 2011

Two months. That's how long I lasted in my second go-round at AllProfile before the dreariness of the job dragged me down. I hated what I did, the people I worked for, the people who worked for me, and those damn cigarettes I was smoking in the parking lot.

I wasn't supposed to be there.

You know when someone gets arrested and people say things like: "He didn't stand a chance. He grew up poor, his dad was never home, he didn't have the opportunities other people do." Well, I am the "other people" in that story. The person who had the upbringing the bad apples missed.

As a kid, I was smart, driven, and likeable. I scored a 1460 on my SATs back when they were out of 1600,[9] went to college

---

[9] If you ever want to know how to spot the guys who didn't get laid in high school, look for the ones who still remember their SAT scores.

on a partial academic scholarship, and graduated with honors. I was raised by two loving and supportive upper-middle-class parents, and I'm a white, heterosexual male. The only way in which I'm at all an outsider is that I'm Jewish. And let's face it, no one looking at the list of folks running Fortune 500 companies would call my people a disenfranchised minority.

So when I graduated college, I never thought I'd end up at a job that left me feeling so simultaneously gross about myself and bored out of my mind.

Back then, I was sure this was exactly where I wouldn't be. I was going to have a job that was fun and challenging and fulfilling. And anything but ordinary. A month after getting my degree, I headed for Hollywood. I had taken some theater classes in college and been in a few performances back home in Boston, so I was confident I had all the tools needed to become a world-famous thespian.

I assumed that once I got there I'd pay my dues playing bit parts like Coffee Barista No. 2, then eventually get my big break and start booking roles with things like lines and solid paychecks. But over the next couple of years, I learned that most actors in LA would kill for the role of Coffee Barista No. 2.

I spent the majority of my time waiting tables and auditioning for aspiring filmmakers' side projects that were "definitely going to be huge on YouTube."

When I found the notices for these auditions on casting websites, the pay was described as "resume and reel," which was shorthand for, "This is something you could list on your resume that will also generate good clips to include in a demo reel of your work." In other words, you'll be doing this for free.

Furthermore, the audition was always for a film that no one

would have heard of if I ever did put it on a resume, and for some reason they never gave actors a final copy of the project for their reel anyway. If I was really lucky, the notice would read, "resume, reel, food, travel," which meant they would also give you something to eat (usually from the nearest fast food restaurant) and reimburse you for mileage (which never actually happened).

Most of the time this was academic, as I wouldn't get the part.

Eventually, I decided to pull a Sylvester Stallone. I would write and star in my own film. I spent two weeks drafting a story about an actor who discovered he didn't want to be an actor anymore before realizing my script was about me.

At that point, I would still have happily taken a job as a full-time performer; after all, it was a fun way to earn a buck. But I realized I didn't *need* it. It didn't fill my soul the way the guests on *Inside the Actor's Studio* said it should. The way I felt getting up every day to work on the script, that was the way I wanted to feel when I went to my job. Acting was fun, but what I loved was writing.

So I packed up my stuff, trekked back along the same cross-country route I so excitedly took on my way out to Hollywood, and returned home to Boston, where I picked up the only job I knew I was good at: waiting tables. I figured it would cover expenses while I pursued my true passion. And then I proceeded to write absolutely nothing.

Writer's block is something I may never fully understand despite how much time I've spent with it. It's just something that happens. A wall that pops up in front of you and makes you say, "This isn't going to work today, but I'll get to it tomorrow."

Then one day, months have passed, and all the while you've been stuck in park, and what the hell is wrong with you, and why can't you change? And then you don't.

Instead of sitting down to the blank page, I stayed out after work until three in the morning, lazed around the next day, and then headed in for a night shift where the other servers and I talked about all the great places we were going, undaunted by the fact that we were doing nothing to get there.

After a year of serving food, I deposited $100 in an online poker account because I was bored. Then I started winning. $40 here, $50 there. Hundreds turned into thousands, the World Series happened, and what was once an ardent hobby transformed into an obsession. I left my job, and I started earning my entire income playing cards online. It was everything I wanted acting to be: a source of income I actually enjoyed that also gave me the freedom to do the other things I was passionate about.

I constructed my ideal daily schedule: writing in the morning, Texas hold 'em in the afternoon, hanging out with friends at night. I couldn't imagine anything better.

But again, I proceeded to write nothing. Every day, when I sat down at the computer to compose my masterpiece, my mouse ended up drifting over to the poker site, and I started in on the card-playing portion of my day early.

Then Black Friday happened, and there I was, shell-shocked and contemplating my less-than-stellar resume.

Professional Actor: Fail.

Professional Writer: Fail.

Professional Poker Player: Fail.

If I'm being honest with myself, part of why I took that position at AllProfile was because I liked the title. Sure, Assistant Regional Manager was about the most middle-management-y label out there, but if I was the Assistant Regional Manager somewhere, then I didn't have to be the loser who ended up broke and unemployed when online poker went bust. I could be the person who oversaw people and branches of a company that presumably had enough people and branches to need some form of regional management. I could be on a ladder heading to something bigger. And it worked, too.

One day, while out with a friend, I ran into Wendy, a co-worker from a previous job. She was maybe 30 years my senior, and, in our time together, she had assumed that supportive, almost-maternal role older colleagues sometimes take on. She saw me the way I wanted to see myself: as someone special. When she asked me what I was doing, I was glad I was able to tell her that after Black Friday, I had dusted myself off and quickly become the Assistant Regional Manager at some company she had never heard of.

As she looked at me, beaming with admiration, I hated myself. I hated myself for helping her believe that I had the kind of employment worth being proud of. She never could have guessed I was lying to earn a paycheck.

"You really are something," she told me, and she meant it in a good way.

I knew she was right, in a bad way.

But at least I could add a new line to my resume.

Assistant Regional Manager at a duplicitous company:

Exceeding expectations.

Around the same time I started at AllProfile, I picked up a shift one night a week with a company that ran trivia games at bars and restaurants. They dispatched hosts like me to various places that were looking to bring some extra customers in the door. I would go to my venue, hop on a microphone, ask trivia questions, play music, and give away prizes, all the while helping the people in the room have an enjoyable night out with their friends. The feeling of fun this new weekly gig gave me was the exact opposite of what I got from my day job.

So when a couple of months at the market research company had me looking for an exit, I decided to pitch the head of the trivia company on the idea of my working five nights a week for him instead of just one. I figured that the money I earned there, coupled with what I made doing odd jobs and some disciplined spending, could be enough to support myself. I'd be doing something fun and leaving plenty of time for writing.

It was a moment of pure joy when my trivia boss's e-mail came in agreeing to my proposal, followed quickly by utter dread as I prepared to tell my market research boss that I was quitting. Just like I had two years earlier.

After only two months on the job.

"Nah, man. This isn't happening," he said when I told him. "You're not fucking me again."

I'd like to say Rick was being unfair. But he wasn't. When I applied to rejoin the company, his superior expressed concern about bringing back someone who had already jumped ship before, but Rick had gone to bat for me. Declared that things would be different. That I was actually interested in sticking around this time. And now I was reneging.

Yes, I was miserable at AllProfile, but I had known I would be when I took the job. And yes, Rick had misrepresented the percentage of my day that I could spend on the couch, but I had a hunch that was how things would be before I ever started.

"I'm sorry," I said. "My boss offered me this opportunity, and it sounds pretty awesome." I didn't think it necessary to bog Rick down with pesky details, like the fact that this was all my idea.

"So you're abandoning me?"

I couldn't say I blamed him for feeling betrayed. You know that line, "It's not personal, it's business"? It's wrong; business is personal. And the only reason Rick ever hired me was because we were pals.

"I'm not abandoning you." *Yes, I am.* "I'm giving two weeks' notice, and I'm ready to train whoever replaces me. But this is practically my dream job. And I would hope that, as my friend, you would want me to take it."

"Dream job? Doing what? Hosting trivia and writing? That's not a career!"

When we met years ago, Rick had talked about how he wanted to be a painter. He was good, too. He showed me his work once. But he had long since quit the whole art thing. Now it was simply a silly hobby he once had. Which meant he was everything I feared becoming: a sellout plugging away at a monotonous nine-to-five, living for the weekends. And I was everything he was so glad not to be: a starving artist who refused to grow up.

He continued, "You're not going to become some famous author. They're going to give me a promotion soon, and then you'll be the Regional Manager and get my salary. Don't you want that?"

Then he said it. And it wasn't one of those moments where the words slip out and you realize you just hurt your friend and you swear it came off the wrong way but now you can't take it back. He meant every ounce of it.

"Or are you gonna keep being a loser for the rest of your life?"

I think I had a response. A line I fired back. But I don't remember it.

I had been thinking about that word "loser" a lot lately. It seemed like an apt term for someone like me. And I couldn't help but wonder if, 20 years from then, I'd be 45 and doing this same dance. Working crap jobs, living in a cheap apartment, eating ramen for dinner, all while I pursued some unrealistic career because I couldn't accept the fact that work isn't always fun. Hell, even in that moment, I was quitting to give myself more time to write despite the fact that, aside from a few sustained bursts of effort at different junctures in my life, I had never demonstrated any real discipline in the area.

Yet 25 seemed like an awfully young age to give up on being a dreamer. So I stood my ground, refused to take back my resignation, and insisted that Rick was wrong. That I wasn't going to be a loser the rest of my life.

Though the whole time I couldn't help but wonder if he was right.

Odd Job #5: Blood Donor

How I found the gig: Craigslist

Time worked: 30 minutes

Pay: $100

Both sides take a leap of faith when it comes to answering a Craigslist notice. The job posters are trusting that the person who responds will show up and do the designated task, while the person who responds is trusting that, when he arrives, the job posters won't tie him up and sacrifice him to their underworld god, Zotan. If you've ever been on either side of a Craigslist listing, you know that both of these expectations are optimistic.

In this case, a company called BioBlood was offering $100 to draw 100 milliliters of my blood. And while I could certainly use the $100, I have a general life rule that if some Craigslist rando wants to stick a needle in my vein, I'm not just going to take it on faith that he is legit. I'm neurotic like that.

My investigation, however, didn't alleviate my concern. The Better Business Bureau had no record of the company, and Yelp had zero reviews. And if you've ever been on Yelp, you know that's saying something.

I was torn. On the one hand, I wanted the $100. On the other hand, this was how most kidnapping movies starring Liam Neeson started. So I gave the company a call.

"Well," explained the secretary, "this is a sterile, professional environment, and we use brand-new needles for every patient. Everyone on our staff is thoroughly trained and has an average of six to ten years of experience in the phlebotomy field."

"Okay," I said. "Is there anyone you can refer me to outside the company who will attest to all that?"

"Um… well, we are on Facebook." *Well that is quite the credential!*

"You got anything else?"

The woman on the phone had told me that BioBlood was located on Main Street, right next to St. Mary's Hospital. If you're like me, when someone tells you they're performing medical procedures right near a hospital, you assume they're in some way associated with said hospital, and not, for example, located in what appears to be an abandoned shack that happens to be next door.

You would be wrong.

The parking lot pavement looked like it had been ripped by an earthquake, stray trash was scattered everywhere, and the building's splintered glass window was held together by Scotch tape. It not only looked bad, but it also wasn't the best endorsement of the decision-making abilities of whoever thought Scotch tape was strong enough to ensure the window's structural integrity.

I braced myself for the worst as I opened the door. *If it's a crack den, I run. If it's a crack den, I run.*

But instead, I walked into a room with carpeted floors, beautiful furniture, and a plasma TV on the wall. Most impressive of all, the magazines in the waiting room were from the current month.

I signed some forms and was taken to a back room by a woman named Helga, who sported a thick German accent. Before that day, I had assumed that all women named Helga with thick German accents were required, by law, to be able to bench press a grizzly bear, eat 30 sausages, and then win a rowing competition after which they would undoubtedly fail the drug test.[10] But this Helga was gentle and thin, with wire-framed glasses hanging from a cord around her neck.

As she asked me questions, I gazed around the room, grateful that it looked like a real doctor's office. There were rolls of gauze, fancy instruments, and a bed covered in butcher paper. While the boxes labeled "blood and stools" were mildly disconcerting, they did at least seem like something a legitimate lab might have.

"Now, I need a small sample for the centrifuge," Helga said. *Centrifuge? As in, what they use to train astronauts?*

She pricked my finger with a needle to draw some blood, which she placed into what I presumed was the centrifuge. She flipped a switch, and a loud whirring sound like a factory turbine started up.

"What's your height?" she shouted over the roar of the machine.

"About six-foot-two," I shouted back. *What the hell is happening to*

---

[10] My kind of woman!

my blood right now?

"Weight?" she hollered.

"195!" I replied.

She stuck a thermometer under my tongue, glanced at the output, then wrote down 34.7 percent on her paper. *Did she just put a percentage for my temperature?*

The centrifuge spun to a stop, and she checked the readings. "Oooh, you just made the cut. You're at 34 today." *Thank goodness. I felt more like a 32.* "Now, we'll be drawing 100 milliliters of your blood, a bit less than they take when you donate with the Red Cross. Is that okay?"

"Yeah, that's fine. I've given blood before."

"Okay. You sure? Because this can hurt." Helga asked this question or one like it four or five times. To the point where I began to worry how much of a wimp vibe I gave off when I met new people.

Then a big, strong woman came in the door. Now *she* looked like a Helga.

"Hi, my name is Daisy," she said. *Of course it is.* "I'll be drawing your blood today."

Once she stuck the needle in my arm, she looked over at me and asked in a deeply concerned voice, "You doing okay? Does it hurt?" Then she made a wincing face like she was experiencing sympathy pain.

"Yeah, I'm fine."

A few minutes in, she looked over again, tilting her head as she spoke. "You are doing so well." *How much do they coddle the patients who aren't 6'2", 195-pound men who have given blood before?*

Once we finished, Helga offered me a cup of pineapple juice while Daisy clamped the line they had used to draw my blood.

"You said I clamp here? And here?" Daisy asked Helga, as though she was still learning. This is always what you want to hear from someone who recently finished plunging a needle inside you: uncertainty about what they're supposed to be doing.

"I don't need any juice," I told Helga.

"Okay." Helga shrugged and tossed the cup into the sink. The same sink where Daisy was currently working with bags of my blood.[11]

"Oh! Juicy blood!" Daisy shouted.

"Ha!" Helga exclaimed. "Juicy blood!"

They shared a laugh like this was the kind of thing that happened so often it was becoming an inside joke.

When we were done, they gave me my check and led me to the exit. And that was it. Aside from the restriction that I couldn't give blood for 56 days, I was done.

I didn't think much about the experience until two months later, when I got a call from an unrecognized number.

"Jonathan! It's Helga!" Helga exclaimed like we were old friends.

The name rang a bell, but I couldn't quite... "From BioBlood! *BioBlood... BioBlood...* "Do you know why I'm calling?"

"Well—"

"We need more blood!" she shouted. Her tone was the kind someone uses when announcing that you've won the grand prize for being their 10,000th customer.

---

[11] I should say that, in their defense, the bags were sealed closed.

Then the memories came back. The frightening parking lot and the woman who supposedly had six to ten years of experience asking if she was doing the procedure right.

"Though I should tell you we have moved," she said. "And you may notice our phone number is different." *You moved, and your phone number is different? Why do you sound like you're on the run from the cops?* "But don't worry, we still pay $100."

"I'll be there."

Odd Job #6: Ghost Writer

How I found the gig: A website called TaskRabbit, where people post projects they need done, and folks like me submit bids for the price at which we'll do them

Time worked: 1 hour

Pay: $7

"I was recently laid off," Peter Randall's notice explained. "A neuropsychiatrist I worked for says he has 'super high praise' for me and would like to write an amazing letter of recommendation... but he wants me to write it." This was where I came in.

Just like his boss, Peter Randall didn't want to write the letter of recommendation, so he hired me to do it for him. On behalf of the man who was apparently so overwhelmed with high praise that he couldn't contain himself long enough to document it.

Peter had been given a blank-check reference, and rather than putting in a small amount of time to capitalize on this significant opportunity, he decided to hire someone he had never met to craft the letter explaining who he was. It is possible that decisions like this were part of why he was laid off.

While it was clear that the reference shouldn't laud Peter for his ability to "complete simple assignments without assistance," he did have some very impressive strengths. At least, according to him. He sent me an e-mail with bullet points covering what I should say, a few of which I have included below.

- I was working at a private neuropsychiatric clinic as a medical historian (interviewed patients and gathered medical history for the neuropsychiatrist).
- I am not sure what work I want to do next, but I just want to be armed with a good letter from this doctor. Dr. Thompson says he has "super high praise" for me and would like an amazing letter of recommendation for me.
- Like how this sounds: Rarely do I have the pleasure to meet someone with the ability to connect with a myriad of people on a personal level through intelligence, charm, and an eclectic education that ranges from.......[12] Furthermore, his creative capacities far exceed that of the majority of people that are of his age and experience, which is paramount.....[13]

---

[12] I have got to imagine that taking the five seconds to list those subjects of study instead of putting an ellipsis and leaving me to guess would have been a good use of Peter's time.

[13] Paramount because why? Paramount because why?! This is like in the movies when the guy is bleeding to death from a gunshot wound and says, "Remember, the most important thing is to never..." Then he gasps for breath and goes limp.

- Responsible, diligent, honest.[14]
- Stayed on task til job was finished and stayed overtime as needed.[15]

Peter then encouraged me to craft the letter however I saw fit, saying, "You are free to do whatever you feel is best. I trust your judgment."

I didn't know where Peter had gotten such blind faith in a total stranger who was unsuccessful enough in life that he would take an assignment that paid only $7. But I dare say, I think Peter was right. Between the bullet points, my follow-up questions, and some educated guesses on the day-to-day responsibilities of a medical historian for a neuropsychiatrist, I put together a sterling endorsement for the services of one Peter Randall. By the time I was done, even I wanted to hire him. He came off as focused, thorough, creative, competent, and a dedicated team player.

When I sent him the final version, he was blown away.

"Thank you so much," he told me. "I will recommend you to all my friends."

I smiled, certain he would not. But hey, maybe he could hire someone to do it for him.

---

[14] I assume this is not counting the time he hired someone else to falsify his letter of recommendation because he didn't feel like going through the effort of creating one himself.

[15] Clearly.

Odd Job #7:
Research Study Participant

How I found the gig: Signed up on a university website to be contacted when they needed subjects for studies

Time worked: 2 hours

Pay: $24

    The research study started at 7 a.m., which meant I had gotten up at 5:30. Add in the fact that we weren't allowed to bring coffee into the room, and I was already in a bad mood.
    Then I met Pink Scarf.
    Pink Scarf was a ball of energy and enthusiasm that any sensible person who had barely slept the night before couldn't help but detest. And she laughed at everything. Like, everything. At some point, she told me her name, but I didn't care. Learning your name is a favor I reserve for people I like. She was wearing a pink scarf so that would be her handle.
    "I'm Jonathan," I said into a microphone a research assistant had placed in front of me, and Pink Scarf laughed like I had told a brilliant joke. Vintage Pink Scarf.
    For this study, a university team would be observing as Pink Scarf,

two other people, and I worked together to complete a series of tasks. And before we could begin, we had to introduce ourselves and test the microphones that would be recording us.

Next to test the sound equipment was a quiet girl in an Oxford shirt, another introduction that elicited a laugh from Pink Scarf. After her was a disheveled guy wearing athletic pants. He looked like the researchers had woken him up from a nap he was taking on the sidewalk ten minutes earlier when they realized they were still short one participant. His hair was a wreck, he looked ready to nod off at a moment's notice, and even I—someone who had worn the same sneakers and hoodie every day for virtually two years—felt he could have tried a bit harder.

"Is this thing on?" Athletic Pants said into his mic, and Pink Scarf absolutely lost it. It was all she could do to keep from rolling on the floor. Everyone else was there to do a study and get paid. Pink Scarf was looking for something more. Like maybe some new BFFs who would make each other mix CDs and friendship bracelets.

"Over the next couple of hours, you four will work together on what will ultimately amount to 31 challenges," explained the woman leading the study. *Can we vote someone off after the first one?*

"Those computers," she said, motioning to the laptops in front of each of us, "create a sort of collaborative workspace. Anything one of you types will be part of a document that everyone else can see and edit."

After taking a few moments to familiarize ourselves with the computer system, we were given our first task. We received a long passage of text and were told to type as much of it as we could into the shared document in the allotted time.

"I'm a slow typer," Pink Scarf said. "I think someone else should type."

"Well, we can all type onto the screen," I said, explaining the process we had been introduced to literally seconds earlier. "Maybe each of us should type a different portion of text."

The passage popped up in front of us.

"I'll type the first paragraph," Oxford Shirt volunteered. I liked Oxford Shirt.

"I'll take the second," I said.

"I'll do the third," said Athletic Pants.

"Which should I do?" asked Pink Scarf. *I don't know, the seventh?*

"How about the fourth?" I suggested.

Oxford Shirt and I plowed dutifully through our paragraphs. To the surprise of no one, Pink Scarf's fingers moved across the keyboard mildly slower than tectonic plates. And most frustrating of all, Athletic Pants had screwed up and accidentally placed his cursor directly in the middle of my paragraph before typing, intersplicing his text with mine.

"Does everyone want to make sure they're typing in the right place?" I asked, not wanting to single him out.

"We are," everyone answered. I stared at Athletic Pants. *Really? You think the third paragraph starts in the middle of the second one?*

"Okay, I only ask because it looks like the third paragraph may have gotten a bit jumbled."

"No, I've got the third one. It's fine," Athletic Pants responded. I stared at him with a hatred that surprised me. Forty seconds later, we were running out of time. Ten seconds. Five. "Wait. I think I did this wrong," Athletic Pants announced.

Seriously?

The task ended.

We navigated through some more typing exercises, then came a five-minute multiple-choice quiz on pattern recognition.

"I think the first one is C," said Oxford Shirt as the test began.

"I agree," I said.

"And the next one is D," she said.

"Yup," I said. "And three is C."

"Ooh, yeah it is."

The two of us moved in sync, racing through the questions.

"Ten seconds," Athletic Pants announced.

"I think I got the first one." Pink Scarf told us. *I hate you.* "Oh wait, we already have the first one." *Yup, that's the one we figured out first.*

"Yeah, we're on the seventh one now," I explained.

"Oh."

We progressed from task to task, with Pink Scarf finding a way to do something frustrating on each one and Athletic Pants threatening to break a Guinness record for inactivity.[16]

As we sat looking at a grid of images for task number 21, Pink Scarf spoke up. "Man, we should be getting paid more for this."

Some of us should.

"When I do these studies at Harvard," she went on, "they usually pay like $50."

"Yeah," Athletic Pants responded, passionate for the first time all

---

[16] If you're like me, at some point you begin to wonder if Pink Scarf and Athletic Pants were plants, made to test our reactions as they confounded the process. I guess I can't say for sure, but from talking to them in the hallway afterward, I am confident they were being themselves and were indeed regular volunteers just like me and Oxford Shirt.

day. *You're saying that getting the amount you agreed to before you began isn't going to cut it?* "Or, like, normally, they pay you more if you do better on the tasks, and then you have an incentive, you know?"

Believe me, you do not want to be compensated based on performance.

"That's what I'm saying. An incentive," Pink Scarf echoed.

As Oxford Shirt and I continued to do all the work, the other two spent their time complaining they weren't making enough for everything they weren't doing. The process continued until our final task of the day: imagining a scenario where we had been in a plane crash and were the only survivors on a desert island. A desert island that would most likely take search crews three days to find. At this point, I could imagine no worse fate.

We were shown a list of items we recovered from the wreckage and instructed to rank the items in order of importance to our survival. The list included four gallons of water, four silk scarves, a first aid kit, gasoline, a machete, a shotgun, whisky, matches, a handheld cosmetic mirror, cheese, a compass, and several other things.[17]

"All right! I'm good at this stuff," Pink Scarf told us as she rubbed her hands together with anticipation.

Good at what stuff? Surviving on a desert island for three days after a life-threatening plane crash?

---

[17] It occurred to me that there were several additional questions that also needed to be asked, like, "Doesn't the fact that someone brought four gallons of water and four silk scarves on board a plane that ended up having *exactly* four survivors seem like something Homeland Security should look into?" And, "How did no one in TSA catch THE PERSON BOARDING WITH A MACHETE?"

"The water is pretty important," I said.

"And the cheese is the only food listed," said Oxford Shirt.

"What are we going to do with the cheese?" Pink Scarf asked.

I know what we can do with the shotgun.

"Well, that's the only food we have," I repeated.

"Oh. And don't forget the whiskey. We can have a good time with that," she told us.

You're right, you are good at this survival stuff.

"The mirror doesn't seem that important," I said. "We could probably rank that towards the bottom."

"We can use that to signal the rescue crew," Pink Scarf said.

"We're going to flag down the rescue plane flying thousands of feet above us with a handheld cosmetic mirror?" I asked, forgetting to keep my sarcastic thoughts internal.

"Yeah, you can make a powerful reflection with those," Pink Scarf explained.

"Yeah," Oxford Shirt nodded. *Wait, did Oxford Shirt just side with Pink Scarf? I was devastated.*

"Okay, let's put the mirror towards the top of the list," I conceded. Maybe a pocket mirror could hail an airborne search crew. Who was I to disagree? After all, it was something I had never tried to do before. And come to think of it, I had never used a handheld cosmetic mirror either.

We finished the study and were paid our $24 (though not without some futile haggling by Pink Scarf), then made our way out of the room.

As we walked towards the elevators, Pink Scarf offered to help us get into the studies at Harvard. This was unfortunate because I really enjoyed hating her.

"They're easy, and they're fun," she chuckled.

Why was I so hard on both her and Athletic Pants? Sure, they didn't carry their weight, but our success on these tasks ultimately meant nothing, so why did I care? Pink Scarf was friendly and joking in the way that she knew how, while I was being an arrogant prick about a pair of people who weren't as good at brain teasers as I was.[18]

I smiled and said goodbye, making a mental note to apply for studies with Harvard next time. Ideally ones that required a little less teamwork.

---

[18] Several friends told me after the fact that they agreed with Pink Scarf's assessment that we needed the mirror's light-projecting capabilities. I cannot tell you how aggravating this was to hear.

Dream Job

November 2011

Reading that last post years later, I was surprised at how nasty I was to Pink Scarf and Athletic Pants. And I considered not including it in this book.

Storytelling 101: Don't write an unlikeable protagonist.

But I couldn't leave it out. What I wrote reflected an important part of what was happening at that time: I was not a happy person. The odd jobs and trivia were not covering expenses, so I put the rest on credit cards. No paycheck remained in my bank account for more than a day or two. On multiple occasions, I nearly came to blows with people who ordered the most expensive item on the menu and then couldn't understand why I was the only guy at the table who had a problem with splitting the check evenly.[19]

When I received bills, I was never able to cover them all, so I paid only the most urgent ones, leaving the rest for some day when I might have more money. I prayed companies wouldn't discontinue my various services, in large part because I feared the embarrassment of those around me realizing just how bad my situation was.

When they cut off my cable, I frantically called Comcast, desperate to get the matter resolved before my roommate came home and tried to turn on the TV. When they cut off my phone line, and I got an e-mail from my mother saying there must be an issue with my number since she couldn't get through, I dashed off a response that maybe there was a glitch with T-Mobile's service and I would check it out, then had to go lie down from the overwhelming sense of shame.

Some of the odd jobs I did turned into recurring work. I started working with a market research recruiter who would call me sporadically about studies that needed participants. I began giving blood at a new clinic whose window remained intact even without Scotch tape. And after getting a desperate phone call from someone I used to act with looking for another performer for a show that week, I joined a dinner theater troupe that put on murder mystery shows. These different activities paid a good rate for the time invested, and after a lifetime of hearing dinner theater mocked, I was shocked to discover how enjoyable it was. But those were still scattered pieces of income that added up to maybe a few hundred dollars a month. Even when you factored in the money I was making hosting trivia five nights a week, it

---

[19] I still hate those people.

still wasn't nearly enough.

Far more of my employed hours were spent on things like that research study with Pink Scarf: twenty-four dollars for two hours doing something boring on the other side of the city.

I eventually moved out of my apartment when I couldn't afford it anymore. On my blog, I talked casually about how it would be fun to crash on different friends' couches. It would be like a sleepover every night. Plus I'd stay at my parents' house for a few weeks, and it would be nice for us to have a chance to spend more time together.

But being four years out of college and still unable to make rent did not feel good. And sleeping in my childhood bedroom when I was broke didn't feel like the choice of someone hoping to see mom and dad more. It felt like the last resort of a guy who couldn't get his life together.

If I wanted to play Freud, I would speculate that the reason I cared so much about how I did on those quizzes in that research study was because it was a chance for me to be the smart guy again. In my mind I was an intelligent person, but I doubted anyone would look at my life from the outside and see me that way. A couch-surfing vagabond whose most profitable days come in the form of market research studies and giving blood for money? Yeah, that's someone who's going places.

The more I struggled, the more I wanted some sort of external validation—and the less my life seemed worthy of it. I wrote online about my experiences crashing with friends. It's interesting living with someone for a couple of days. You see what their morning is like when they sleep through the alarm, how they act before drinking coffee, the dirty rooms whose doors they normally close when guests come over for parties. You see them in a more vulnerable state than they usually allow. And I made fun of them on my blog. I made jokes about the things they did in those moments. About the way they kept their apartments. About what they prioritized doing before they headed off to work. I told myself that they would know I didn't mean it. That I teased them all the time, and my writing style was that of a guy cracking wise about the world around him. But teasing your buddies when it's just the two of you isn't the same as doing it on a website read by people they had never met.

Afterwards, one of the friends I had stayed with became more distant, though I had no idea why. She could never make it when I invited her out and never seemed to initiate plans with me. Whenever we saw each other at a party, she was always in the middle of talking to someone else. After awhile, I decided that maybe we weren't as close as I had thought. It wouldn't be until a couple of years after the fact that we would hash it out, and she would tell me how much my blog post about the few nights I spent at her place had hurt her feelings. But at the time, I was too self-absorbed to realize it could possibly have been my fault.

Then there was what I wrote about my girlfriend at the time.

I heavily implied that she had dumped me because she didn't want to stick around for the hard times. In reality, nothing about our breakup had anything to do with her not being there for me. If anything, it was me not being there for her that was the problem. I was too focused on my own stuff, my own life. I was always running from one thing to another, with no time for her. But on your blog, you get to tell the story the way you want it read, so that's what I said.

The more difficult things got, the more myopic my viewpoint became. The more oblivious I was to the other side. You know those people who act like they're the only ones in modern-day America who are busy? That was me. In every conversation, I had to bring up how much I had going on. Everything I got invited to, I either couldn't make it, or I left the person feeling like I was doing them a favor by squeezing them in. When I initiated plans, they were always for when I was going to be in the neighborhood for a gig with a couple of hours to kill. I made time for friends the way you fit in going to the grocery store on the way home.

Despite how little money all my work generated, it still found a way to absorb almost every hour I had. There were also all these hidden time sucks, like how long I spent applying for gigs online. Or the 20-plus hours a week logged commuting, often driving to four or five separate locations in the same day, some of them over 50 miles apart. Or that time when one job ended and the next wouldn't be starting for an hour and a half—not enough time to go home, not enough time to do something else, just a stretch where I had to sit and wait.

Occasionally, there were another ten hours devoted to writing about these experiences, though that was happening less frequently. My perpetual busy-ness wasn't leaving much time for the blog, which was theoretically the impetus to do all this in the first place.

During my few moments of stillness, I slotted the elements of my to-do list into the spaces of my day like Tetris blocks. I'd have 40 minutes to kill between research studies, so I could spend that time responding to all the e-mails from prospective employers. The next day, I would have half an hour between when I finished breakfast and when I left for the clinic to give blood. I could use that block to fact-check the set of trivia questions my boss had sent me because the person who usually did it was sick.

It went nonstop until the moment I got into a friend's bed or foldout sofa, when I would crash into instant sleep from the exhaustion.

Most of the time.

I remember one night, though, staring at the ceiling, a beam in the couch digging into my back and keeping me awake. As I lay there, the thoughts I was normally too busy to notice crept in.

I never expected I'd be this much of a screw-up.

Without a home, in all sorts of debt, cobbling together a scattered set of incomes that didn't come close to covering expenses yet still somehow consumed my entire week.

I couldn't help but think about how I told Rick I was taking my dream job, and he had laughed in my face. It was probably for the best that we didn't talk anymore; he was the type who liked to say, "I told you so."

Then my friend's cat entered the room, hopped onto my chest, and settled in for some rest. Dozing off was going to be hard, but I told myself this would make for a funny joke on my blog.

Odd Job #8: Panhandler

How I found the gig: Went out and did it on my own

Time worked: 25 minutes

Pay: $0

It was supposed to be fun. A sort of experiment. I was going to dress up like a homeless person, panhandle in downtown Boston, then blog about it. I was going to make a few jokes about how my regular outfits were already so bedraggled that I didn't need to buy any special clothes for the assignment, throw in a few more about how itchy my face was after not shaving for three weeks to better look the part, and finish with clever ideas for what to put on my sign. Then, when I was done, I was going to donate the money I made to charity so I could sleep at night. That was the plan.

Riding the train downtown, wearing ripped jeans, a worse-for-wear sweater, and an old winter hat, I concocted a backstory. It takes a certain amount of privilege to think you can get in character to effectively play a homeless person in a mere 20 minutes, but privilege has never been something I've lacked. Sure I'd never spent months sleeping on the streets in the rain and cold, receiving constant looks of disgust and judgment, not knowing if I'd earn enough to tide me over to the next day when I'd do it all again. But 20 minutes? That was plenty.

Imagining myself without a permanent address was easy. After all, I had recently left my apartment and was without a place to call my own because I could no longer afford rent. But when you live in the same city as the one where your parents still have your childhood bedroom set up the way you left it, it takes a bit of imagination to capture the true desperation that comes with being homeless.

I pictured having lost it all to a gambling addiction: left unable to cover the expenses of daily living, struggling to find employment, deciding to beg on the corner for a few days, then a few days turning into a few months. I asked myself what-if questions the way they taught us to in my college acting class. What if I didn't have a safety net or a support system? What if I wasn't white? Or a college graduate? What if I wasn't in good mental and physical health?

I got off the train, walking with a slouch and a what's-the-point face. I passed a street performer playing a keyboard for money and trudged up the stairs into downtown.

I studied the homeless people I passed. Some asked for money, others ranted to anyone who would listen. I had never realized how many of them there were. I came to the crosswalk and stopped next to a kid who couldn't have been more than 20. He sat on the ground with a sign reading "TOO UGLY TO PROSTITUTE" and a cup holding a few quarters and nickels. It should have read "TOO YOUNG TO BE HERE."

Glancing into the receptacles of all the panhandlers that passed by, I was struck by how little they had made. Here we were at 1 p.m., the morning and lunch rushes over, and these guys had barely anything to show for it. Maybe they had spent or pocketed some of what they had collected, but had they all done that? Wouldn't at least some keep change in their cups like coffee baristas seeding their tip jars?

The numbers didn't add up. Every homeless person was begging for money, and every potential donor was walking right by them, eyes locked straight ahead. There was nowhere near enough to go around.

I looked for a place to set up shop. I wanted something out of the way where no one would see me. The 26-year-old who thought this would be fun. But I forced myself to sit down in the busiest spot possible and held out a cup with change and a few dollar bills I had already put inside to get the ball rolling.

Then I froze.

I couldn't get the words "Spare change?" out of my mouth. I again recalled my acting lessons. If students couldn't cry onstage, the teacher would make them beg a classmate for something they desperately needed. Being completely at the mercy of another human being is usually enough to push people past the brink.

What if this were real? What if these people avoiding my gaze were my only hope for survival? What if I had to compete with the dozen homeless people on this city block for everyone else's scraps? What if this was my every day?

My mouth unable to say the words, I took out a slab of cardboard I'd brought with me and wrote my sign: "Spare Change?" I held it in one hand, my cup in the other, still mute. I tried to make eye contact with the people walking by, their pace quickening as they passed.

One woman sat on a bench, eating her lunch, watching me. Studying me like I was a zoo animal. After 15 minutes, she got up, threw out her unfinished sandwich, gave me one last look, and left.

I planned to be there for four hours, but I didn't make it 30 minutes. Though time moved so slowly that it felt like more. I walked over to a stretch of grass and lay down to take a break. I couldn't stand up. I didn't want to go back. I told myself that it would make for an interesting blog post. I reminded myself that I hadn't shaved for three weeks and had set aside the whole day for this. Did I do all that just to sit there silently for 25 minutes, then go home? What would I tell all the friends who knew today was the day I was going to be a homeless man and come back with some great, hilarious story?

It didn't matter. I couldn't make myself do it.

I shoved my sign in the trash, then headed for the train. What a jerk I was to approach this all so cavalierly. Like it would be fun. Here I was, telling myself that my situation crashing on friends' couches was in any way comparable to being truly homeless. I was trying to put myself in the shoes of someone living on the street, while the whole time I knew I had a fail-safe that real homeless people don't: If I didn't like my job as a panhandler, I could quit.

Headhunters

November 2011

"I saw this and immediately thought of you. You'd be perfect for it," my friend Alex excitedly told me as she handed me her phone, the web browser opened to a news article. I started reading, but she couldn't contain herself long enough for me to finish. "They want to give people money for their poop!" she blurted out.

The article was about a company coming to the Boston area called Waste Not. They were planning to pay volunteers to donate their stool several times a week so labs could perform something called fecal transplants which were, I pray, not as gross as they sounded.[20]

---

[20] As mentioned at the beginning of the book, the names of people and businesses in these stories have been changed, and I must admit that a rather

When you start a blog detailing what you do to earn money, these are the kinds of things your friends lead with when you meet up for dinner. Alex was the third person to tell me about this company that week.

People often asked me where I found the jobs I wrote about. There was Craigslist and a then-new website called TaskRabbit.[21]

But there was another channel. When you start a blog, relevant opportunities seem to find you. Partly, it's that the more you think about something, the more you see possibilities you would otherwise miss. And partly it's that the more you talk about something, the more people bring ideas to you.

The guy I played poker with who ran a nightclub was suddenly no longer just a friend but also someone who might be able to hire me for a day. I started reading those random fliers posted in coffee shops and on utility poles. I noticed freelancers and entrepreneurs who built their own thing and

---

significant portion of one of my days went toward coming up with a good fictional title for this company. It is one of my greatest failures as a writer that my friend Greg came up with "Waste Not" and not me. But I am proud to announce that I definitely figured out the perfect slogan for this company: "Give us a run for our money."

[21] At the time, TaskRabbit worked on a bidding model. People would post tasks they needed completed and folks like me would submit bids in hopes of being hired to do those projects. You would say how much you would charge and why you were best qualified for that job. Whenever I saw something that was perfect for the blog, I would underbid the field. The site has since changed its model so that now, when you need something done, you choose from a list of people you can hire, along with details about their rates and credentials.

thought, "I could do that."

I got an e-mail from a friend's sister offering me a slot in a study her lab was running. An old coworker suggested I reach out to her former roommate about demonstrating his company's product in stores. Even my landlord asked if he could pay me to water his plants while he was on vacation.

In fact, if you ever want to increase the number of options you find in a given field, may I recommend writing about it online? You could blog about every band you see, and you would become the person all your friends message when they have an extra concert ticket. I'm sure that those people who share stories about their struggles in the dating world are constantly getting e-mails from readers about prospects who would be "just perfect" for them. Someone named Kyle McDonald famously blogged about his quest to trade a red paperclip for something better, then trade that for something else, and keep on bartering until he ultimately got a house. And it worked. I'm sure many of the offers he received came from people who found his website and thought it would be fun to help him on his mission.

Somehow, I had unlocked this amazing life hack and was using it to get shitty job offers.

Literally.

But it worked. Slowly the gigs piled up, some of them turned into recurring opportunities, and eventually I was making enough to move into a new apartment with a couple of roommates I found online.

Even better, people were reading what I was writing. It felt good when friends told me they had seen the links I posted on Facebook and were enjoying my blog. Some had even forwarded my work to others. My stuff was being seen by an audience I had never met.

Though it did have the unfortunate consequence of meaning that any time I ran into past acquaintances, there was a good chance they knew intimate details about me. Or worse, they had filled in the blanks about the rest of my life with guesswork.

"This is Jon, we went to high school together," an old buddy named Dave told his friends when we randomly crossed paths at a bar one night. We hadn't seen each other in eight years, but I guess he had been following me, because the next thing he said was, "He writes an awesome blog." *Please Dave, you're making me blush. But yes, it is pretty amazing.* "If you ever want to read about a guy who had it all then lost it thanks to a gambling addiction and now has to do terrible jobs just to get by, you've gotta check it out." *Wait, what? Is that what you think I—*

"Oh cool. Sounds like a fun read," said the cute girl in his group of friends who now would never go out with me.

"Well, I mean," I tried to explain, "It's not like I lost it by gambling on... And I wasn't addicted to... And I don't *have* to do these terrible jobs, I choose to... Well, it's not 100 percent a choice but I could just get a regular... Well, more importantly, my life isn't *terrible*... Yeah, I guess just check out the blog."

Others had assigned me the imaginary life of a professional blogger, assuming I was making money from... whatever ethereal source it is that bloggers make money from.

At a reunion event for my high school improv troupe, my former castmate, Heather, eagerly asked, "Is that your full-time job? Writing about the random stuff you do?" The excitement in her eyes was a look all of us aspiring artists get when we meet people who pay their way doing something they enjoy. People who make you think maybe you can do the same. The way she felt in that moment was how I felt when I met the poker pros at the World Series who inspired me to try playing cards full time.

Of course, her perception of me was an illusion. I wasn't the person we both wished I was. The cost of the new apartment had absorbed any extra money I was earning, meaning I was still beyond broke and adding to my debt.

I told her no, this wasn't my full-time job, but in a way that made it sound like I was a lot closer to that fantasy than I actually was. Talking with her, someone who barely knew me, I could pretend. She didn't have to know that I was 26 and considered it a major accomplishment that I could finally pay the rent.

The truth is I was somewhere between the Sisyphean existence Dave had imagined of a man struggling to pick up the pieces from a poker career gone bust and the triumphant one Heather had conjured of an artist living his bliss. On some days I believed I was getting closer to the latter, but on most I was just inches past the former.

It didn't help watching my peers. My best friend and his wife had just bought a house where they could raise their daughter. House, wife, daughter. Three entities I couldn't begin to imagine in my life. It wasn't that I wanted those things, but I had always thought those options would be waiting for me when I was ready. Now I wasn't so sure.

This friend and I had stood at the same starting line when we graduated college, along with almost everyone else I knew. When I left for LA and declined to get a standard nine-to-five, it was sort of like going left while the other runners went right. And with each milestone the people around me hit as my life stayed the same, I couldn't help but wonder if the road I was on would ever meet back up with theirs. Not in terms of the careers they had, but in terms of what came with those careers: financial security, normal schedules, family.

But in that moment, with my old buddy from high school improv, we could smile at how much more fun my course was than everyone else's.

That thing where people funneled job offers my way ultimately helped me get on slightly steadier footing when a friend who knew I was good with her son got me a job as an afterschool teacher a few days a week at the place she worked. I liked kids, plus the regular paycheck shored up my finances significantly. And for that I was grateful.

But it also left less time for my blog. Crazy though it may sound, I liked that my friends were coming to me with stories of poop clinics. Doing new things and having an excuse to write was fun for me, and I didn't like the idea of something else pulling from that.

Taking the afterschool job was like moving half a step in the direction of the path my friends were on, and I couldn't tell whether that was a good thing or not.

Odd Job #9: Afterschool Teacher

How I found the gig: Referred by a friend

Time worked: 10 hours per week

Pay: $16.25 per hour

With the help of a referral from my friend, I picked up a job several days a week at Lawton Elementary in the afterschool program. There was a lot to like about the position. It paid enough that I could finally afford things like rent, and I could eat as many goldfish as I wanted from the food cabinet. Plus, I suppose the kids and I developed a wonderful relationship/connection, blah blah blah, but it was mostly the goldfish thing.

Of course, there were also some issues. Apparently, the meaning of the term "afterschool teacher" had changed a lot over the years. When I was a kid, the emphasis was definitely on the "afterschool" part. As in, the school just wanted a body to throw in a classroom as soon as the regular day ended, allowing them to tell the parents, yes, your child is being supervised. Now, at least in the upscale neighborhood that was Lawton, Massachusetts, the focus had shifted to the "teacher" part. They wanted an educator who could reinforce key concepts from the regular curriculum while also exploring new ones.

This shift manifested itself in a couple of ways. First off, every day we had to lead activities that were both fun and educational, which was a problem since my boss disagreed with my argument that playing Bananagrams and doing Mad Libs every week fulfilled those objectives.

And second, I had to "attend" accreditation courses. These came in the form of watching online videos meant to explain core teaching principles, then taking a quiz at the end to verify that I had absorbed the key points.

Anyone who has ever taken such classes in any industry knows these videos have two defining characteristics: One, they are historically boring. And two, the quiz questions are so easy that you get dumber just by reading them. This was an actual brain buster from one of them: "Poor quality child care is a threat to children's healthy social-emotional development. True or false." I quickly realized that I could press play on the videos, go clean my kitchen, come back, ace the quiz, and print off a certificate of completion.[22]

My plan worked perfectly. Curious how you might fare on these exams without having seen any of the videos? Let's find out. Below are my favorite questions (in bold) followed by the correct answer (in italics) followed by my thoughts (in regular font).

Which of the following are signs of adverse reactions to medication?

---

[22] Note to my former boss if you're reading this: Don't worry, I would never do that. I hate cleaning my kitchen.

A) Difficulty breathing

B) Rash

C) Drowsiness

D) Nausea or vomiting

E) Headache

F) All of the above

Correct answer: F

Because if high school taught us anything, it's that the answer is always "all of the above." The only time an answer will not be "all of the above" is if one of the options is "A and B, but not C." Teachers love that shit.

Not that you need to know how quizzes are usually crafted to identify that *both* vomiting *and* difficulty breathing could be bad reactions to medication. This really isn't a question that demonstrates whether or not you should be allowed to care for children as much as it is one that demonstrates whether or not you should be allowed to leave your house without adult supervision.

What should you do with unused medication?

A) Flush it down the toilet

B) Return it to the parent

C) Throw it in the trash

D) Save it for another child who might need it

Correct answer: B

Perhaps the only thing more frightening than a teacher who doesn't think vomiting, headaches, and shortness of breath are red flags is one who thinks that a student's unused steroidal asthma medication could be the perfect solution to another kid's tummy ache.

Which of the following is NOT a common reason why children engage in conflict with their peers?

A) Self-centeredness

B) Limited social skills

C) Unmet needs

D) Concern for the feelings of others

E) Tiredness/fatigue

Correct answer: D

Thus upending centuries of child-rearing theory that Alex, the school bully, beat up Jimmy, the class nerd, because Jimmy had been looking a little glum lately, and Alex was worried about him.

Which of the following strategies can help promote children's healthy social-emotional development?

A) Treat children with warmth and respect

B) Be responsive to children's needs

C) Create a positive emotional climate

D) Talk about feelings and emotions with children

E) All of the above

Correct answer: E

I just... I can't even...

BMI charts can be used to help determine overweight and obesity in children. Obesity is defined as having BMI levels:

A) Higher than the 85th percentile

B) At or above the 95th percentile

C) At or above the 75th percentile and lower than the 95th percentile

D) Obesity cannot be plotted on a BMI chart

Correct answer: B

Let's overlook the horrific grammatical structure of "help determine overweight and obesity in children" (one of an alarming number of written mistakes on a website responsible for educating educators) and move on to the implications of this answer. In the lesson (a rare video that I had actually watched), we learned that the percentage of young people who are obese has tripled since 1980, which can lead me to only one conclusion: Between the test writers and myself, at least one of us does not understand the word percentile. People being at or above the 95th percentile in weight means that they are among the most overweight five percent of Americans, right? Well, that means that the percentage of people who are obese cannot increase at all, let alone triple. If the percentage of Americans who are among the top five percent tripled, that would mean that the top 15 percent of Americans are now among the top five percent of Americans.[23]

Some of the consequences associated with obesity include:

A) Discrimination

B) High blood pressure

C) Gallbladder disease

D) Impaired balance

E) All of the above

Correct answer: E. Of course.

I'm not crazy about highlighting the idea that discrimination can be a consequence of obesity. It teaches children that if someone is

---

[23] Though I do have to admit, if there was ever a situation for which the mathematicians of the world might consider making a one-time exception for how percentages work, it would probably be to quantify how out of shape Americans have become.

discriminating against them based on looks that they should radically change to avoid criticism, thus instilling the mindset that the problem is—

Wait a second. Did you say, "gallbladder disease"? As in the condition you develop in your 60s? Please, show me the first-grader with gallbladder disease, obesity-caused or otherwise. Are there not any consequences of an unhealthy lifestyle that could manifest before kids qualify for their AARP card?[24]

And who was the person trying to figure out four significant repercussions of childhood obesity who just said, "Screw it, I'm going with impaired balance"? All kids have impaired balance. They're kids. I was stick-thin when I was ten and couldn't walk five feet without crashing into something.

This got to another problem with these online classes. I had a sneaking suspicion they were created by people who had zero experience working with children. The video on healthy eating included this gem about food service: "When possible, allow children to serve themselves. Young children can often select the right amount of food to satisfy their appetite."

Here's a tip from someone who's been in a classroom: If the meal is graham crackers, then every kid will take enough. But when you're serving carrots, you get a room full of children saying, "No thanks, I'm not hungry," followed 30 minutes later by those same kids moaning, "I'm staaarrrvvviiinnggg. When's snack time?" Indeed, these videos focused

---

[24] Wikipedia lists the following as putting you especially at risk for gallbladder disease: pregnancy, oral contraceptives, and estrogen replacement therapy. If your elementary school kids are presenting any of these risk factors, then you've got a lot more to worry about than whether or not they could stand to lose a few pounds.

a lot on theory that sounded good but fell down in the face of practice. And that's the thing about childcare. Some stuff works in scenario A, and some stuff works in scenario B, but very rarely is one particular solution the right choice for all of the above.

Odd Job #10: Brand Ambassador

How I found the gig: Craigslist

Time worked: 8 hours a week for 4 weeks

Pay: $15 per hour

"What is this?" a mousy woman asked as she peered into our display at a local Whole Foods.

"We're called FarmFaire," said Theo, the man I was shadowing while training for my latest gig. "We sell cold-pressed, organic, non-pasteurized juices."

"Oh my. Non-pasteurized," the woman said, placing her hand on her collar-bone. Pasteurization is a preservation method drink companies use for their juices that has the unfortunate tradeoff of compromising some of their nutritional value. Non-pasteurized drinks maintain the health integrity of the beverages while reducing their shelf-life. In other words, making something non-pasteurized is sacrificing some of the product's financial viability in order to maximize its health benefits. At Whole Foods, using the phrase "non-pasteurized" is a mild aphrodisiac.

"Here, try some," Theo said as he poured her a cup.

Our job was to sell FarmFaire product, and Theo was good at his job. He could tell what people wanted to hear, and he knew how to give it to them. This was important because our product was very expensive. Like, $10-a-bottle expensive.

He explained, "It has ginger, which, as you know, has been used for centuries to settle upset stomachs."[25] Internally, I rolled my eyes. *Ten dollars to cure an upset stomach? At that price, I'd just tough it out.* But this sales pitch wasn't for me. It was for her. And she ate it up.

She slurped loudly. "Ooohhh, yeah," she said as though it had settled an upset stomach that, moments before she met us, she presumably didn't have.

"And it's also been found to improve the circulatory system."

The woman sipped again. "Oh, absolutely. Gotta take care of that circulatory system." You could tell she now felt the blood racing through her heart at maximum efficiency. "How much does it cost?"

This is where we lose her.

"Right now, it's only $9.99 a bottle," he said.

Yup, ten bucks. For juice. I know what you're thinking. You're thinking you have mortgage payments cheaper than that. And hey, I don't blame y—

---

[25] Somewhere along the path to eating right, the idea that we did something centuries ago became synonymous with "healthy." I've always been curious how the first advocate of this ideology pitched it to everyone else. "Sure, people used to die at age 25, and medicine was mostly guesswork, but I found an old diary from a guy who used a root to ward off an upset stomach before dying a week later of diphtheria! This stuff is incredible!" Here are some more things that were cure-alls way back when: mercury, bloodletting, and drilling holes in people's heads without anesthesia. I think I'll stick to Pepto-Bismol.

"Great, and which aisle is it in?"
Seriously?

Over the next few weeks, I became an expert myself. I used visual aids to show how much produce we crammed into every bottle. I talked about the cold-pressing and the non-pasteurization and the wonders they did for your circulatory system. By the time I was done, it was hard to believe these drinks were as cheap as they were.

As I talked to customers, I studied the Whole Foods ecosystem. I watched them gush when they saw terms like "organic" and "locally grown," and I watched them recoil when they saw terms like "high fructose corn syrup" and whatever the word is for "non-locally grown."[26]

"Who do you work for?" a slightly older woman asked me one day.

"FarmFaire," I answered. "We're a company committed to selling healthy, organic products made with methods that are both ethical and environmentally conscious."

"Okay." She leaned in closer, fixed her right eye on me, and asked warily, "But who do you *really* work for?"

"FarmFaire. That's the name of the company."

"So, you're not owned by... *Coca-Cola*?" She almost spat in disgust as she said the name.

"Nope, we're an independent company."

"Good." She smiled. Now that she knew I was on her side, she dropped the aggressive tone and spoke like we were old friends. "I met a

---

[26] I believe that word is "affordable," but I'm not positive.

person doing a demo for healthy drinks once, and it turned out that her company was owned by…" she paused to build suspense, though I felt it was pretty obvious at that point that she was about to say Coca-Cola. "Coca-Cola." *NO! OMG!*

"I don't get it," I said. I did get it, but I like to be difficult.

"Well, here they are, claiming to be this healthy beverage company, but they're part of the unhealthiest company of them all." She spoke like she was revealing someone's plot to assassinate the president.

It occurred to me that Coca-Cola probably had one of the largest, if not the largest, drink manufacturing and distribution infrastructures on the planet, which allowed it to offer such low prices. And while FarmFaire was great for the rich shoppers of America, the fact that lower-income people now had access to healthy drink options was a good thing. But I said none of this.

"Oh, wow," I told her. "That sounds terrible."

At first, I mocked. But as I spent more time in these stores, speaking this language, I started becoming one of them. A Whole Foods consumer in every way. Buying their products. Scanning the labels for phrases like omega fatty acids and sodium phosphates, despite having no idea what either of those was. After all, almost everyone who shopped there was educated and beautiful. So, on some level, didn't that have to mean that buying these products was a smart decision that helped you look your best? Meanwhile, the food was delicious.

I started to feel better and generally more awake as I moved throughout the day. I stopped groaning like a 60-year-old when I got out of my chair. I didn't know whether the effects were real or placebo, but hadn't science resoundingly proven that placebos were supremely effective?

And as I became one of them, I realized that more than products that were good for them, people wanted products that they could tell themselves were good for them. That we come to Whole Foods *hoping* to find a drink that costs $10, since just by pure math, it has to be five times as good for us as that crappy $2 drink. Spending $10 on our health means we're making it a priority.

I'm not saying that people don't get healthier eating Whole Foods products. I'm simply saying that I'm guessing there's a gap between how much good these products do and how much good shoppers convince themselves these products do. But maybe the positive feeling that fills that gap is part of what you pay for. And maybe you get your money's worth.

One day, instead of juice, I was handing out bite-sized samples of a self-described "natural energy booster." Personally, I had my doubts. I was on four hours' sleep and had been downing the things like M&M's all morning but didn't feel a difference.

A woman who looked as tired as I felt walked up to me. As I explained the product, I could see from her body language that she thought I was pulling a fast one. That whatever I was selling couldn't possibly cure the exhaustion that had been dragging her down all morning. But she took a handful anyway, skeptically tossing it into her mouth. She eyed me as she chewed, then swallowed.

"Oh my God!" Her face lit up. "I do have more energy. I didn't believe it at first, but this totally works." I watched, speechless, as she happily tossed a bag into her cart.

While I doubted that anything short of snorted cocaine could make its way into her bloodstream as quickly as she thought that food did, it was undeniable that she was no longer as tired as I was. As she walked away, I couldn't decide whether I pitied or envied her.

Odd Job #11: Bikini Model

How I found the gig: TaskRabbit

Time worked: 1 hour (time to buy bikini) + 10 minutes (wearing the outfit)

Pay: $64 + a bikini

This job kept getting worse.

Which was impressive, since, even at its starting point, it had problems.

The starting point was someone named John hiring me to dress up in a bikini and deliver a copy of the *Sports Illustrated* swimsuit issue to his friend.

"This is not a joke, and there's nothing weird," his job listing had read. "Ring the bell, hand him the magazine, and that's it." It struck me as a gross misuse of the phrase "there's nothing weird."

But since first getting the gig, I had learned a little bit more about John. It turned out that he ran a website documenting stunts and pranks performed by him and his staff. And he was intending to record the delivery, then upload the video to his site.

And so as I stood in my bedroom, dressed in nothing but a two-piece, staring into the mirror, one thought kept repeating itself over and over in my head: *Why did I apply for this?*

The backstory was this: Last year, John's friend Brandon never got his swimsuit issue—the once-a-year *Sports Illustrated* magazine in which they stop talking about zone defense and instead show photos of hot women in bikinis[27]—because his wife, Brenda, grabbed it from the mail before he got home.

She gave it to their mutual friend John and asked him to build some sort of fun stunt around delivering the magazine to her husband. So John placed an ad looking for a bikini-clad woman to show up at Brandon's door and personally deliver the issue. An ad to which I responded by pointing out that this would be a lot more interesting if he hired a bikini-clad man who had enough chest hair to be mistaken for Big Foot. John agreed.

But now I was having second thoughts. Not because my fat was sticking out in an awkward tuft several inches above the bikini bottom. And not because the polka-dot pattern had looked way better in the store mirror.[28] But mostly because I didn't know who the hell this John guy was.

---

[27] You're not going to believe this, but this is, every year, *Sports Illustrated's* best-selling issue.

[28] Walking through the aisles of Target, holding options against my body to gauge what might fit, was one of the more awkward moments of my life. Carrying multiple swimsuits into the changing room was a bit more difficult. But the most uncomfortable part came when a store employee informed me that if I couldn't find anything I liked, there were some additional options in the plus-

What if this is actually a prank John's pulling on me? What if John's friend is the chief of police and I get arrested? What if John knows my outfit's lack of pockets will force me to leave my wallet in my car, and he's going to take my money while I'm at his friend's door?

I ultimately decided that none of these was worse than the what-if I had already resigned myself to: What if I show up almost naked at some random guy's house, then get photographed and videotaped for a story that ends up on the World Wide Web?

I put on a pair of knee-high black socks and white shoes that I felt completed the ensemble, then tossed on some jeans and a hoodie that I would wear until I got to the elementary school near Brandon's house.
Oh, did I not mention that John had asked me to meet him at an elementary school before heading over to Brandon's? Like I said, this kept getting worse.

John explained that the reason he had chosen the school as our rendezvous point was that we needed some easily identifiable landmark near Brandon's house in an otherwise non-descript residential neighborhood, and this was the only option. I suppose his logic was sound, but I have this personal hang-up about coming to a grade school with less than a foot of fabric covering my body. Call me a prude.

Luckily, it was the weekend, so I figured no one would be around.

Of course, I was wrong.

---

size-and-maternity section. I mean, I already felt self-conscious enough, but then she had to call me fat?

A construction crew was there renovating the building. Which was good, since if there was anything I less wanted to walk by in this outfit than a school full of children, it was a construction crew.

Seeing John pull up in his car, I was surprised by how normal he looked. After all, when you know an adult has committed his life to running a website featuring stunts like this one, you kind of assume he'll look like that guy in your freshman dorm who you weren't positive went to school there because you never saw him go to class. But John was a handsome man in his 40s with a sensible outfit and a sensible car.

"The bikini's on under my clothes," I explained.

John glanced at the construction workers and nodded. "Probably a good idea."

"So, what's the plan?"

"Well, Brandon's 50th birthday was last week, and we're going over to celebrate."

As John spoke, he nodded at the people in his car. I glanced over his shoulder at a Volvo that I now noticed was loaded with his wife and two kids. *Wait, why are there kids here?*

"It'll take us a few minutes to get there, then give us another ten to settle in," John continued. *Why are there kids here??* "We'll say hi, sit down, have some cake with his family, then you come to the door and hand him the magazine." *Why are there kids he—wait, did he say "family"?*

"Wait, did you say 'family'?"

"Yeah, just Brandon's wife and children." *How many kids are going to be at this thing?!*

The drive from the school to Brandon's house was a short one. And now, as I waited in my car, I was struck by how unstoppable time was. Each moment I looked at the clock, it was later than the moment before. I was irrevocably moving closer and closer to something that until now had only felt like an abstract idea and not a real, live thing that was going to actually happen.

Nine minutes. Six minutes. Two minutes. One minute.

I pulled off my hoodie and pants, then stepped into the middle of the road. The top was stuffed with tissues to help fill out an A cup, and the elastic band on my bottom was holding on for dear life. I prayed Brandon's neighbors weren't the kind that liked to look out their windows.

Or go outside.

I walked up Brandon's front steps, my stomach doing nose dives as I rang the bell. *God, do I hope I got the house number right.*

Brenda was the one who opened the door, and, judging by her reaction, I'm guessing John hadn't told her exactly what he had planned. It was the closest I had ever come to seeing a human being's eyes pop out of their sockets.

Then came the scream. The sort of noise you thought was only made by birds in the Amazon during mating season.

The families came pouring into the hallway to see what was wrong. John, his wife, four kids still in grade school and, of course, Brandon. The victim.

I walked up to Brandon and calmly began my concocted story. I explained that I was with *Sports Illustrated*, and we had recently discovered that a block of subscribers never got their swimsuit issue. *SI* was rectifying the problem by sending people in bikinis to hand-deliver copies to any customers they had missed.

If Brandon had asked why a man and not a woman was at his door, I had a whole paragraph ready to go about how, due to fears of discrimination lawsuits, they had hired a staff that was half male and half female. But he was too dumbstruck to speak.

As I talked, I could see everyone pulling out their cameras, including John, who was recording the whole thing.

I walked Brandon through the issue, flipping through the pages and pointing out some of my favorite models.

"Would anyone else like to see?" I turned to the rest of the group.

"No! The kids!" screamed Brenda. Somehow the 6'2" yeti of a man with barely any clothes on was fine, but seeing those sultry photos would have crossed a line.

I smiled and thanked them, then headed for the exit. Soon my picture would be posted online, and I would officially never be able to run for president.

Sometimes that's what it takes to ensure someone has a 50th birthday they'll never forget.

It seems that it would be unfair to spend all this time discussing what I looked like and then not show a picture. However, it occurs to me that seeing a hairy man in a poor-fitting and revealing ensemble might not be what you signed on for when you started reading today. So if you're curious, simply flip the page and look. If you're feeling modest (or if you're related to me), focus your eyes hard to the right, perhaps using your left hand as a blinder when you turn the page. But remember that whichever option you choose, it was your decision. Not mine.

I knew you'd look.

Odd Job #12: Depressed Research Study Participant

How I found the gig: Craigslist

Time worked: 2 hours

Pay: $20

    A little past Harvard Square, Massachusetts Avenue forks twice in the span of ten seconds, which was usually enough to inspire a nervous breakdown in my GPS. Despite the fact that I had driven this stretch of road a thousand times, it continued to confound me as much as it did my navigational system.

    You would think that just by guessing which way to go, I would get this right at least occasionally, but I never did. I somehow always made the wrong turn. And going to this odd job was no exception. I guessed incorrectly and ended up heading away from my targeted location in Cambridge and towards Somerville—a different city altogether that probably owed half its population to people who were trying to get to Cambridge and took a wrong turn. I spent 15 more minutes swearing loudly and turning down side streets before I finally reached my destination: one of the many boringly named buildings at one of Cambridge's more prestigious universities.

As I stepped out of my car, I had a weird feeling of déjà vu. I had been here for a research study before. I got lost and swore a lot on the way the last time, too.

I met the girl administering the study, and we walked into the lobby. "Just to warn you, the elevator's been acting crazy lately," she explained nonchalantly as we got in. "Hopefully, nothing goes wrong." *Wait, what?*

The doors closed.

"Are you a student?" she asked. I was now two years into my *Odd Jobs* experience. That's two years of doing these studies and two years of empty conversations beforehand. They always asked if I was a student. I didn't know whether it was because I looked young (the positive interpretation) or because most college graduates weren't free at 1 p.m. on a Tuesday and jumping at the chance to do a two-hour study that paid $20 (the more realistic interpretation).

We walked into the room, and it dawned on me that I hadn't just been in this parking lot, in this building, having this conversation before. I'd actually done this exact study before. Eight months ago.

Before we began, she asked a series of questions meant to gauge to what extent I was or was not depressed. The hypothesis of their research was that people who were suicidal or depressed had slower reaction times than people who were not.

It was possible that universities had run out of things to study.

My answers came out automatically, with my brain barely paying attention to what she was asking. No, I don't have an eating disorder. No,

I don't have thoughts of suicide. Yes, I feel happy.

But then one of her queries caught my ear. "Do you ever feel like you're going nowhere in life?" And I paused for a moment.

I'd always felt like I was going somewhere. Like I was scraping by for the moment, but someday it would all be worth it. I would become a full-time actor or poker player or author and be my own boss. And those years bussing tables and doing shit work to make ends meet would be worth it. Lately, though, I hadn't felt that way. I'd felt like maybe this temporary rut wasn't so temporary.

"Yes," I heard myself answer.

Because this was a research study, she then asked the same question 20 different ways.

"Have you felt like you were going nowhere in the last three months?"

Over the last three months, any routine I had developed with my blog had almost completely atrophied. I was barely ever posting new content. I was always too busy, too tired, too something. When I started *Odd Jobs*, the goal was to put up something new every Friday. Then it became every other Friday. Now, I was going weeks at a time without creating anything.

I felt gross when I didn't write. Like the way you feel if you don't shower or change your clothes for a few days. I had done this before. Where I had been writing every day and feeling amazing, and suddenly stopped for no apparent reason and felt miserable. The novel I had started a couple of years ago, the random short stories I had put online as part of my pledge to upload a new one each month, or those times I tried to launch a blog about playing poker.

You may say, well, then why not just start again? And of course you'd be right, and I had no idea why I didn't. I only knew that on some days, staring at a blank page and trying to fill it up with words felt like trying to lift the world's heaviest boulder, and so I hadn't been doing it.

"Yes."

"Have you felt like you were going nowhere in the last month?"

I'd been picking up extra gigs all over the place, but it was an hour here and two hours there with an hour of driving in between. I had no regular schedule, and my sleep cycle had gone to hell. While I enjoyed hosting trivia and performing in murder mystery shows, some of the other stuff was painfully boring. I was always stressed, often miserable, and I didn't see a way out.

"Yes."

"Do you feel excited about the direction you are going in?"

Part of why I created my blog was to do new things. To get away from the tedium of the nine-to-five world. Yet now even these odd jobs felt the same. Hell, I had literally done this exact study before.

There was the occasional escapade in a bikini which, despite my bellyaching, I enjoyed. It was exciting and different, and it got me back in front of my keyboard. But those exotic gigs were rare diversions in what had become a steady stream of dull research studies and random errands.

"No."

"Do you feel excited about where you will be five years from now?"

"Go fuck yourself." (I didn't say that.)

As the questions rolled on, I slowly realized that in this study comparing depressed patients with non, I was being slotted into the former column, not the latter. Then she gave me a series of mindless tasks that my brain tuned out as they passed slowly by, like scenes in a boring movie. When it was all over, she handed me a $20 bill. We both said thank you and nice meeting you. Then I left.

As I crawled through traffic on my way home, I thought thoughts I had had at many points in my life. I am happy when I write, why am I not writing? I want to quit my day job, this time the one at the school. I always quit, then suddenly realize that I need more income. I am tired of feeling like this.

I felt like I was driving down Massachusetts Avenue. I had been here a thousand times before, and I always made the wrong turn.

Side Hustle

July 2012–April 2013

Composing the "Depressed Research Study Participant" post was a surreal experience. It was like my brain was using my keyboard to work through feelings I didn't know I had. I hadn't noticed how much of a rut I was in until I not only participated in the experiment, but also typed up something about it. I certainly hadn't understood how much not writing was putting me in that rut.

 I always knew I enjoyed writing, but I enjoyed lots of things. I enjoyed cheesecake and watching football and playing poker. Drafting that post helped me realize that writing did something more. It left me fulfilled and happy in a way that extended beyond the time I was physically at the computer. The way seeing the girl you love lifts your spirits and then keeps them elevated long after she's left the room.

The days where I felt bummed or distressed, those were the days I needed that feeling the most. So "Depressed Research Study Participant" became a sort of manifesto: Keep writing.

Writing was something I had only done sporadically over the years. And while any graph of my dedication had its peaks, it was mostly valleys. One peak came when I launched the *Odd Jobs* blog, and that felt good. But slowly my commitment to posting something new every week faltered, and my blog went through long stretches of inactivity interrupted only occasionally by rare bursts of inspiration.

I have always looked for turning points in my life. Those moments, like in movies, where something big happens, the music starts pumping, the training montage kicks in, the protagonist starts running in the streets, and he transforms from zero to hero. When I haven't been able to find them, I've manufactured them. Looked in the mirror and said, "As of today, I'm going to start writing every day," or some similar declaration—a pledge that usually didn't survive through the end of the week. I had made these fast-vanishing resolutions in other areas of my life, too, always with the same results. So while I believed at the time that that blog post would be my cue-training-montage moment, there was still a voice in my head that was certain I'd be wrong.

But I wasn't. Something was different this time. Something made me actually change. It wasn't as clean a transition as in the movies. My training montage still featured scenes where I skipped the gym and ate a donut. But overall, I was improving.

And when I found myself relapsing, I would think back to that study and what I had learned: that putting pen to paper made me feel better, more complete. And I'd get back in front of the blank page.

It was a three-steps-forward, two-steps-back, stumbling march, but I could feel myself slowly leaving the valley behind.

And something else happened right around that time. I started picking up a new category of jobs, ones where I was actually paid to write.

John, the man who ran the website that I had dressed up in a bikini for, read my *Odd Jobs* blog, liked it, and asked if I wanted to do stupid things and chronicle them on his site.

For pay.

Ummm... Hell, yeah!

After a few attempts at a recurring feature where I prank-called different companies' customer service numbers, I eventually found my groove writing articles about my adventures completing random challenges like listening to a country music radio station for 24 hours straight or spending the entire day taking a bath (both of which were better choices than some of the other options my editor proposed).[29]

Early the next year, in April of 2013, bombs went off near the finish line of the Boston Marathon, only a few miles from where I was at the time. I wrote about it on my website. It wasn't an odd job, but the blog had developed an audience, which meant

---

[29] My editor once sent me an e-mail detailing several different stunts I could try. They included calling my mom and telling her I had secretly been in love with her for years, the all-day bath article I ended up doing, and one option that simply read: "Ax-Wielding Hitchhiker." When I asked what that last one was, he matter-of-factly replied, "You stand on the side of the road trying to hitch a ride while holding an ax." What? You don't get those e-mails from your boss?

it was a place where my stuff would get read. People I had never met shared it with their friends. My words were touching readers outside my social group.

A week after that, an editor for an online magazine who saw the piece reached out and asked if I wanted to submit an article to her, which turned into an opportunity to interview my favorite radio personality, Peter Sagal. If you're not a 65-year-old NPR nerd, you'll have to take my word for it that it was pretty cool.

Slowly, more and more of the hours in my day were spent getting paid to do the thing I loved. And in those hours, I wasn't someone stringing together random gigs to make ends meet.

I was a writer.

Odd Job #13: Mickey Mouse

How I found the gig: Referred by an actor in the murder mystery troupe I had joined

Time worked: 3.5 hours

Pay: $100

If you're not from Massachusetts, you probably know the Battle of Bunker Hill as "Wait, which one was that again?" But here in Beantown, we can't find enough ways to celebrate it. At current count, we have a monument, a bridge, and a day off from school, which is all the more impressive when you consider the fact that it was a fight we lost to the British.[30]

And then there's the parade. A celebratory march held on the Sunday before June 17, honoring the most successful loss in US military history with floats and firetrucks and Miss Massachusetts winners.

---

[30] The story goes that the English forces were so badly depleted by the Battle of Bunker Hill that they realized a few more wins like this one, and they would lose the war. Which sounds to me sort of like when your 5-year-old loses the soccer game, and you lie and tell him that winning isn't everything, but whatever.

A couple of months earlier, I had started working with a company called BirthdayBash that typically provided actors dressed as superheroes and Disney characters for kids' birthday parties. The characters played games, posed for pictures, and helped families ring in their child's special day in style. The job came by way of a referral from a fellow member of the dinner theater troupe who, when I expressed a fear that I would spend the whole time in some uncomfortable costume getting kicked in the shin by obnoxious tikes as they chanted, "You're not real," shrugged and replied, "Yeah, but it pays well." Fair enough.

And now, since BirthdayBash had the costumes and the actors anyway, the city had contracted us to march in the parade, dressed up as a few of those characters. Namely, Spiderman, Cinderella, Mickey Mouse (that was me), and Mickey's girlfriend/sister/platonic-roommate/I-have-no-idea-what-their-relationship-is Minnie Mouse.

Like most people, I grew up adoring Mickey. As a kid, I wore the fake mouse ears so often that the hat formed a symbiotic relationship with my scalp.[31] I watched his shows and read his storybooks. I even

---

[31] Photographic proof from a time when I was still cute:

convinced myself that *Fantasia* was a good movie.[32] So when I first got the assignment, I was excited. Right up until the moment I saw the costume.

While Mickey Mouse represented the innocence and joy of childhood memories, the Mickey Mouse costume more closely represented the agony and trauma of enhanced interrogation techniques.

My bad back struggled with the fake head, and, within minutes of arriving at the parade, my cheek developed an itch I had no way of scratching. Meanwhile, the costume combined with the 90-degree day to create a level of heat usually only experienced in small nuclear meltdowns. But the biggest problem was the lack of vision. Apparently there is an industry-wide directive for mascot heads that eye holes should line up perfectly with the performers' chins and provide zero peripheral vision. This outfit was made to spec.

As we stepped into the parade and began marching, though, all that faded away. I no longer cared about the discomfort as unadulterated adoration from the spectators poured over us.

Suddenly, we were the Beatles coming to America. The newly crowned Super Bowl champions returning home from victory.

People cheered and shouted that they loved us. They stormed the parade to take pictures with us and exchange high fives. The people on the sidewalk let out warm "awwww"s as children hugged us with all their hearts. It felt good to make kids' days, to be revered, to feel the applause of a couple thousand fans.

For that short window, I knew what it was like to be a celebrity.

But as the day wore on, the parade ran long, and we fell behind

---

[32] That's right, I said it.

schedule. The directive came for us to pick up the pace, and suddenly we didn't have time for one-on-one interactions with folks in the crowd.

~~Luckily, everyone acted rationally and completely understood that we couldn't pose for pictures with every single person on the side of the road because, ya know, that's not normally how parades work.~~ People went apeshit.

"MICKEY! JUST STOP FOR ONE PICTURE!!" shouted a parent.

"Mickey! What the hell?! You don't have time for a little kid?"

"Sorry folks," Spiderman told them. "We gotta keep moving."

"No! You really don't!" yelled an intoxicated resident who apparently had a better handle on the parade schedule than the marchers.

People hurled insults and obscenities. Parents literally ran down the street for several blocks to catch up with us, then forced kids into our arms for photos, not even pausing to make sure we had firm grasps on their children in our awkwardly oversized gloves.

Clearly not caught up enough, the parade accelerated even more. Suddenly, we were running. I nearly trampled several small boys who I didn't see rush into my path. The vitriol grew louder.

With the admiration of the surrounding masses no longer distracting me, the feelings of heat and weight came rushing back. My brain spent the next 40 minutes triggering every single pain receptor in my back, and my thin, felt shoes, combined with racing on the pavement, left the bottoms of my feet screaming for help. Meanwhile, a gig that was supposed to be two hours had stretched to three-and-a-half.

By the time we returned to our starting location, I felt like I had been through the Battle of Bunker Hill myself. We ducked into a side parking lot, pulled off our costumes, and downed about a gallon of water each.

As we waited for our ride, our bodies covered in sweat and our psyches frazzled, I marveled at how fast love had transformed into hatred. Somehow, I had gone from the most beloved symbol of American childhood this side of Santa Claus to the a-hole who couldn't take two seconds to give a kid the photo op of his dreams.

Factor in the heat and weight of the costume, and I was ready for the day to be over.

As great as it was to be my childhood hero for a few hours, I was grateful when I finally got to take the mouse ears off.

Odd Job #14: Balloon Artist

How I found the gig: Went out and did it on my own

Time worked: 6 hours

Pay: I lost $70

    The real victims of the time I learned how to make balloon animals were my roommates. Our apartment overflowed with deformed monkeys, hats that would only fit the most asymmetrical of heads, and guitars that looked like elaborate strap-on dildos.[33] The constant nails-on-chalkboard screech of balloons rubbing against each other was only interrupted by the gunshot bangs of them bursting. Though perhaps even more

---

[33] No, seriously:

annoying was my habit of giving away my practice creations as gifts.

"Thanks," one of them would say, trying to be polite as I handed him what looked like a mutilated horse in need of a nose job.

"It's an elephant," I would explain.

"Oh, I can tell," he would reply, in the way that parents tell their children that of course they know exactly what's being depicted in their art class drawings.

Then we would stare at each other awkwardly as I waited for him to tell me how impressive it was that I was making so much progress and as he wondered how long the rules of politeness required him to keep this thing before he could throw it out.

For two weeks, the apartment was my laboratory. I poured over YouTube how-to videos and churned out practice creations. Dozens of flowers and puppies stacked up beside my chair as I tossed my finished designs to the side and started new ones. The math seemed simple enough. If I set up shop in a busy public venue and cranked these out at $2-a-pop with the occasional $5 or $10 tip thrown my way by a generous patron, a full day of balloon twisting could easily yield $200.

At 11:30 a.m. on a beautiful Thursday in August, I arrived at Boston Common, a public park in the heart of the city, ready to launch my career as a balloon artist. I set up shop at the Frog Pond, a pool of water about five inches deep and populated exclusively by children, probably because kids are the only people with active enough imaginations to dream up a scenario where five-inch-deep water could be fun.

The children splashed around with their friends, while their moms and dads sat strewn on the sidelines with that war-torn-refugee look all parents get when they've made the disastrous decision not to send their kids to summer camp.

It was a literal teeming pool of potential customers. I set up my stool and made some demo balloon animals, planting my tip hat beside me. Then I wrote out my offerings on a dry erase board, blaring phrases like "GIRAFFES!!" "PRINCESS WANDS!!" and "GUITARS!!"[34] All that remained was to wait and let the business roll in.

And so I waited.

And waited.

I tried to stay positive, but it was impossible not to notice that no one was coming over. I could almost hear the parents mind-melding, sending group messages like, "Don't you dare go over to him. If you buy one then they're all going to want one, and I'm going to wind up shelling out 15 bucks for a few swords that will pop inside of ten minutes, and next thing I know, my beautiful day will be filled with crying and broken latex, just like my prom night!"[35]

My optimism slowly faded. My estimates of $20 an hour plummeted. That I had positioned myself amidst a herd of my target demographic and was making nothing was bad enough. But even worse, with each passing moment that no one spoke to me, I seemed less like a street vendor and more like a creepy guy sitting on the outskirts of a pool full of half-naked children just hanging out. It was only a matter of time before what's-his-

---

[34] I should clarify that by the time I got to the children's wading pool, my guitars were looking far less phallic.

[35] Or so I imagine.

name from *To Catch a Predator* showed up to cart me away.

At around the 40-minute mark, a woman mercifully approached me with her daughter. "Can she have a flower?" the mother asked.

Yes!! Yes, you beautiful, wonderful person, I could hear my brain shouting as I turned to her. "Of course."

I inflated a long green balloon and, with a few simple twists, turned it into a perfect stem with elegant leaves extending from the sides. I handed it to the little girl to hold while I pulled out a pink balloon for the petals. "What brings you to Boston Common?" I asked, determined to be not only an expert balloon artist, but also a charming conversationalist.

"We're visiting from Connecticut."

"Oh, wow, you came all the way from Connecticut just for some balloon animals?" I joked.

The woman stared at me blankly, her face unchanging.

This was my best material.

"So, you like flowers?" I asked the little girl.

"Yeah," she said, her face as stony as her mom's.

Good. Definitely nailing this charming conversationalist part. I lowered my head and kept twisting, then handed the child her finished creation. I have to say, it looked good.

The mother gave me $2 in exchange for the flower. "Believe it or not," I told her as I took the money, "you are my first-ever customer. I've never done this before." Again, her face remained a stone wall as she nodded. It appeared that she did, in fact, believe it. She then walked away.

Over the next few hours, I made a sale or two, but things were slow. I also began to suspect that flies are attracted to rubber. Bugs were settling on my balloons and swarming around me. But these were the least of my problems.

"Hey man, can I get one?" a guy asked as he walked up to me. I instantly got the vibe that he was messing with me, but who was I to turn down business?

I inflated a balloon. "What would you like?"

"Just the balloon is good," he said and took it out of my hands.

"You're supposed to tip him," his friend grunted as he walked up beside him.

"Tip him? Man, I ain't got no money for no balloons." I was beginning to regret my pay-what-you-want policy. "But don't worry," he turned to me, "I'm gonna make this into something fly, and then it'll be like advertising, and you'll get mad business." *Did he just use the words "fly" and "mad" as unironic adjectives?*

The man made a twist or two that left the balloon looking basically like it did before only with a bit of a knob at the bottom. He then held it against the base of his pelvis and started thrusting excitedly. Somehow I didn't think this would be quite the boon for business that he predicted.

"Ya gotta do more to get peoples' attention, man," he said as he continued to thrust. "Dance around or something."

Yeah, that's my problem. If only I was dancing like you are right now, this whole venture might finally take off.

"Thanks. I'm thinking of changing locations, seeing if I have more luck somewhere else."

"Yeah, that's smart, man, you should totally try somewhere else." *Oh, believe me, you're definitely selling me on the idea of leaving this spot.*

Seeing that both he and the flies were going to be there awhile, I packed up my gear and headed for the aquarium, which was a short drive from Boston Common.

Until that moment I could still delude myself into thinking I could turn things around and make this a profitable trip. But as I paid my garage fee ($18) and mentally added that to the cost of the stool ($20), balloons ($20 more), dry erase board ($7), and lunch ($15), I couldn't deny the reality any longer.

The aquarium didn't go much better. I spent about ten minutes telling kids that no, I had no idea how to make a lobster or a penguin, before a police officer came along and informed me that I wasn't allowed to hang out on the sidewalk at the entrance to a private establishment, soliciting business from children without a permit.[36]

My day was a waste. Worse than that, I had finished in the red. I threw my stuff into my car and plopped into the driver's seat. Perhaps there wasn't quite as much money in the balloon game as I had thought.

---

[36] Freaking government, man.

Odd Job #15:
Professional Basketball Player

How I found the gig: Recruited by the gym teacher

Time worked: A little under 30 minutes

Pay: $8

    I don't even know what the kids and I were working on. With a month left in the school year, we were hardly trying with our teacher-led activities anymore. But whatever it was paused for a moment when the gym teacher came bursting into our classroom. She was desperate for people to fill out the staff side in the student-faculty basketball game. I glanced at the other teacher I worked with, giving a look that said, "Can I?"

    My fellow instructor smiled back. She was just as checked-out as I was. "Let's all take a field trip to the gym to watch Jonathan play in the basketball game!" she announced, and the kids cheered. They hopped to their feet and formed a line. As I walked out of the room to change into gym shorts, a thought crossed my mind. I was still getting paid for this hour of participating in the game. That meant I was about to become a professional basketball player.[37]

Aside from the technicality of getting paid and having the objective of putting a bouncy ball through a hoop, there was little about the faculty team that resembled a professional basketball squad. Mr. Milton, the chemistry teacher, was already gasping for breath from the pregame practice shots. And Mr. Reagan, from the English department, had braces on both his knees and a third one on his shin—a place I didn't even know people put braces. At 27, I was the only player under 30, and perhaps the only one who had exercised all year.

While our team left something to be desired, the game was clearly ours to lose. Lined up across from us was the eighth-grade varsity girls' basketball team that would be our first opponent of the day (our second would be the boys' team in a game immediately following this one). And while the girls were probably better at pure basketball fundamentals like shooting, dribbling, and being able to run the length of the floor without needing a hit from an oxygen tank, it was clear those advantages paled in comparison to the fact that we were twice their size.

As I glanced back and forth between our team and theirs, I wondered how we planned to make sure we didn't humiliate our opponents in front of their peers. Were we going to duck whenever they shot? Score on the wrong basket? Intentionally pass to them?

---

[37] With afterschool teaching paying $16.25 per hour, and me playing a little under 30 minutes, the yield for my professional basketball career came to $8. Not a lot, but still more than any scouts would have predicted I'd make if they had seen me in high school gym class.

But before we could discuss any such plans, the game was beginning, and a 13-year-old girl with pigtails was dribbling up the court and calling out a play. Her teammates ran with military precision to pre-assigned spots, and she zipped a pass to the open player who took a step-back jumper. And in that moment, it occurred to me that we were up against a group that had spent the entire year practicing and playing together, and maybe we weren't going to waltz in here and annihila–

WHAM!! The French teacher leaped into the air and unleashed a thunderous, Dwight-Howard-like block, drilling the ball halfway across the gym. Another teacher blitzed down the court, picked up the loose ball and completed the easy layup. The answer to the question "How would we go easy on a team of middle-school girls?" had been answered with authority: We wouldn't.

I checked to see if my colleague who made the initial block, and did everything but give the Dikembe Mutombo finger wag afterward, felt any contrition. But he was smiling from ear to ear. Meanwhile, the one who had completed the play was doling out high fives to the kids in the crowd. We weren't going to beat the girls, we were going to embarrass them. I glanced at the student spectators who roared their approval like bloodthirsty fans at a gladiatorial match as the staff soaked in the adoration. For the faculty, this was their Super Bowl.

The thing was, none of us were all that good at basketball. We simply carried ourselves like we were. The next ten minutes were a rarely seen combination of showboating and ineptitude.

One teacher tossed the ball off the backboard to himself, apparently intending to catch it in mid-air and slam home a dunk. Which I guess meant he got so lost in the moment that he forgot about his bad knee. He leaped about three inches off the ground as the ball sailed back over his head. Another teed up a shot from several feet beyond the three-point line, then held his follow-through triumphantly, only to see the ball fall half a foot short of the basket. No-look passes sailed out of bounds and between-the-leg dribbles clunked off of thighs.

Still, we fought hard for rebounds, swarmed on defense, and hunted down every loose ball. As the game clock ticked down, the scoreboard read 16-2, which, when you think about it, tells the whole story. That we gave up only two points in a ten-minute game tells you that we showed no mercy. And that we scored only eight times in those ten minutes of showing no mercy tells the rest.

As the buzz of winning wore off, you could see the grind of the game taking its toll. My teammates were leaning over and panting heavily. The aches were settling in.

"Okay!" the gym teacher shouted. "We're going right into game two."

Oh, no! Game two! My head spun around as the boys' team marched onto the court. They were spry and cocky. Chomping at the bit, eager for a chance to humiliate their professorial overlords. I looked back at my teammates who, in their minds, were already busy scheduling post-game appointments with their orthopedists. Suddenly, playing all-out for the last ten minutes wasn't only poor sportsmanship. It was poor planning.

The next game moved faster than the first. The boys flew across the court, made hard, dirty fouls, and strutted after every basket. We pulled heavily from our first-game strategy, particularly the "be a lot taller than them" play. But the results weren't as impressive.

With six minutes left, we were trailing and fading fast. A fitting comeuppance for the display we put on in game one. But it turned out we had one lower level to stoop to.

The call went out to our bench, and in came a sub who had only recently shown up. He was 25 and had certain things the rest of us lacked. Things like biceps, a functioning cardiovascular system, and talent. And no one seemed to be mentioning the elephant in the room: I had never seen this guy at our school. I think he was dating one of the younger staff members.

We had brought a ringer to a student-faculty basketball game.

Without even warming up, our new teammate started doing his best Bugs Bunny impression. Covering every player on the court and making insane shots look easy. With his help, we hung on for a 16-15 victory, narrowly avoiding the defeat we so badly deserved.

When it was over, we limped off the court and back to our classrooms. It was 3:30. There were still two hours left in the afterschool program's day, and we had to get back to teaching our kids the proper way to behave.

Odd Job #16:
Bathroom Attendant

How I found the gig: Suggested by my sister

Time worked: 2 hours

Pay: $9.04

The bathroom attendant.

The annoying guy manning the sink in the restroom. He's there to help you in that moment when you've finished relieving yourself and it's time to clean your hands. You may recognize this as a point in the bathroom experience for which you need no assistance. But he does not. For him, it's his time to shine. He cranks the faucet, hands you a paper towel, and offers you a mint. Then he stares at you awkwardly until you tip him.

For two hours one day, this was my job. To be the man in the bathroom hoping you'll tip him for a service you definitely don't need.

Here's what happened.

1:45 p.m.

My shift began.

No one had hired me, and no one knew I was coming. The plan was to get in and get out before anyone realized I didn't actually work there. My sister had suggested I try this for my blog after seeing a woman do the same thing—set up her own personal attendant station and work for tips. Some older sisters use their extra years of wisdom to guide their siblings toward choices that maximize their chances for a good life. Mine had encouraged me to solicit business in a men's restroom without the consent of the property owner.

1:46 p.m.

I pulled supplies from my backpack and laid them on the counter top. Hand sanitizer. Floss picks. Mints. Candies (Starburst). And, of course, paper towels. I glanced in the mirror. At home, a white button-down shirt and black tie had seemed like the perfect choice. But this restroom lay adjacent to a giant food court. With toilet paper strewn on the ground and the tiles wet with what I could only hope was sink water, I was clearly overdressed.

1:47 p.m.

My first potential customer. "Paper towel, sir?" I said, but he darted around me to use the hand dryer instead. "Paper towel, sir?" I asked another man who did the same. I was officially requesting payment for a service that was worse than the free option immediately next to me.

1:53 p.m.

"Fresh paper towel, sir?" I found myself asking a patron. *Fresh paper towel?* I internally reprimanded myself. *Really? Throwing the word "fresh" in there is going to change things?* The man smiled and took the towel. *Wait, seriously?*

"Fresh paper towel, sir?" I asked another patron who also took it. I was a genius! Sure, something I had shoved into my backpack and then held in my sweaty palms wasn't technically "fresh," but I wasn't here to create an honest marketing campaign. I was here to move product.

2:10 p.m.

My first tip! "Thank you, sir!" I told the man, overwhelmed by his dollar. "Please, help yourself." I waved my arm over my array of supplies like a pauper trying to impress the king by offering up his possessions. *Want a dental floss pick even though there's nothing in your teeth? How about a mint that's been exposed to the open bathroom air for several hours?* He took one look at my collection and said, "I'm good." Then he left.

2:40 p.m.

I was up to $4 in tips. With each contribution, I found myself taking more pride in my workspace. I wiped down the granite around my station, and I tossed out stray toilet paper. I even started closing all the stalls so that when someone thought they were taken, I could play the hero and say, "This one's available, sir," before opening the door onto an empty toilet.

2:45 p.m.

"Ummm... what are you doing?" The question came from a little boy and his brother, both staring up at me, confused as to why I was there. I like talking to kids, but I felt weird being chummy with a pair of children in a restroom. Especially with their parents nowhere in sight.

"I'm just helping to improve the guest experience at these facilities," I replied. I hoped that by giving the most boring answer possible, I could shut this line of questioning down.

"Is this your job?" he continued. I was expecting the question at some point, just not from someone whose voice hadn't yet cracked.

"Sure."

"So, someone is paying you to be here?"

I was hesitant to lie, but I also didn't want to risk giving myself away to two potential blabbermouths. "Well, I receive tips from patrons."

"But like, are you here because you want to be here?"

"I absolutely want to be here." If my goal was to avoid coming off as creepy, I was failing.

His next question was harder to evade. "Is there one of you in the women's room?"

"I guess you'd have to check to find out." *Did I just encourage them to go explore the women's room?*

The two eyed me like a pair of cops trying to decide if they had enough evidence to take me down to the station. "Come on, let's go," one of them said.

"Okay," the other responded, still watching me over his shoulder as they turned.

I just hoped that when they saw their parents, they didn't start talking about the weird guy in the bathroom who offered them free candy.

3:08 p.m.

A man came in who had used the stall about an hour earlier. My years of restaurant training kicked in, and I instinctively flashed him the kind of warm smile you give repeat customers. A creeped-out look immediately spread across his face, and I realized, a bit too late, that maybe the hearty "welcome back" facial expression was a bit out of place in a lavatory.

3:20 p.m.
"Hey! You work here?"

I turned around, looking for the question's source, but no one was there.

3:21 p.m.
A little louder this time. "I said, 'You work here?'"

The question was coming from the stall behind me. Though I didn't know whether it was a staffer or just a curious urinator.

"Not technically."

"That's what I thought. Ya know, they don't usually like people doing that kind of thing." Aside from my one run-in with seven-year-old Lennie Briscoe and his partner, no one had given me a hard time about being here. Maybe it would be wise to leave before I met an adult who wasn't quite so lenient.

Then the door slammed open, and a man walked out who looked like he'd had a few.

"That's smart, brother." He seemed genuinely impressed. "It's a good hustle. Really good idea."

I looked down at my basket. Nine dollars for two hours' work. Agree to disagree.

"Thanks," I said.

He washed his hands and I gave him one of my last paper towels. He dried off before unwrapping a cherry Starburst and tossing it in his mouth. The whole time he wore a look on his face that said he was thinking hard. "Yeah, real smart," he said to himself.

Then he threw some loose change into my basket. "Sorry, brother, it's all I have."

"No, I appreciate it," I smiled.

As he walked away, I glanced at what he had left me. Four cents.

It wasn't much, but considering the hundred or so people who had used my towels and given me nothing, it was also hard to say he stiffed me.

3:25 p.m.

As I handed someone my last paper towel, I checked the time. My parking meter would be expiring soon. I packed up my stuff, and as I walked out the door, I glanced at the row of urinals. I kind of had to go, but 100 consecutive minutes were more than I ever wanted to spend inside a public restroom. Rather than lengthen my stay, I decided to hold it until I got home. There might not have been a gentleman waiting for me with paper towels when I was done, but let's be honest: Nobody really wants that guy there anyway.

Career Change

May 2013

The portion of each day spent teaching was shrinking, and the portion spent telling the students to just go run around outside and try not to kill each other was lengthening. The weather was getting warmer, the calendar was running out of school days, and then one afternoon I felt it. Something I hadn't experienced since childhood. That uncontainable excitement as four simple words ping-ponged through my brain: Summer vacation is coming.

You could see the enthusiasm on all the teachers' faces. They discussed their upcoming schedules like soldiers who knew the war would soon be over. They talked of travel, time with their partners, and never-ending rounds of margaritas. When they asked me what I had planned, I told them I was going to be working. And I couldn't wait.

Some of that work would be in the form of writing. I had started contributing a regular column to the humor website I worked for. We named it "The Workout Novice," and for each article I would immerse myself in a different fitness fad, then write about it. I did paleo for two weeks, tried every exercise documented in a *Men's Health* magazine, and took up strippercise—a form of aerobics modeled after exotic dancing.[38]

Meanwhile, other parts of that work would be in the form of entertaining. There was still trivia hosting and the mystery shows, plus I was doing more for BirthdayBash. I know dressing up in costume for kids' birthday parties doesn't sound like the best job. In fact, the only reason I originally signed up for it was because I figured that, yes, it would be miserable, but at least that misery would yield a fun story for my blog. But it wasn't miserable. For my first event, I dressed up as a firefighter[39] and

---

[38] Word to the wise: If you ever want a strip club bouncer to think you're cool, don't ask for a receipt for your tax records when you pay the cover charge.

[39] Side note: Even if the party hadn't gone well, it still would have been worth it. That photo of me in a firefighter outfit was a total game changer for my online dating profile.

helped a four-year-old have a birthday he'd never forget.[40]

In addition, working these jobs, I was meeting other performers who would throw random fun gigs my way. Like leading a chocolate tour of Boston or donning a fat suit, wig, and makeup to become Santa Claus at Christmastime.

Even better, a few hours performing at kids' parties or hosting occasional chocolate tours paid as much as several afternoons a week at the afterschool program. When you added everything together, I could drop my job at Lawton Elementary and still make enough to cover my expenses, all while leaving a lot more of my hours free for writing.

The timing was perfect. The head of the afterschool program had sent out an e-mail announcing that budget cuts were coming, and not everyone would be back next year (happy summer!). I think she had figured out the same thing I had: while I loved kids and enjoyed playing games with them, those weren't enough to outweigh how much I struggled at maintaining discipline and running a classroom. However, unlike poker, the job I was forced to leave, or AllProfile, the job my boss resented me for quitting, here both sides were ready for things to end.

Besides, it was only a matter of time before one of the students discovered Google and found a picture of me dressed in a bikini or my article about modeling my cardio routine after the moves I picked up studying exotic dancers. Once either of those

---

[40] Side note to the side note: It was a very different kind of game changer when said dating profile, unbeknownst to me, automatically uploaded a photo from another party of me dressed up as the Incredible Hulk. For fear of copyright violations, I have not included that photo here, but trust me, if you saw me in that costume, you almost definitely wouldn't swipe right. And if you did, you would be sorely disappointed when you met me in person.

happened, I probably wouldn't be allowed within 500 yards of an elementary school anyway.

When I e-mailed my boss to say thank you for everything, it had been great working there, but I had decided not to return the following year, I assume she took it the way my high school football coach did when I told him I was leaving the team: utter indifference mixed with a little relief that I had saved him the trouble.

So it was that on a May afternoon, as the children played outside, I wasn't so much watching them as I was picturing the upcoming new chapter in my life.

"Jonathan!" one of the kids shouted, interrupting my daydream. "Can you play Jonathan Monster with us?"

"Sure!"

I smiled. Jonathan Monster was what it sounded like: a game where I chased the kids like a monster as they alternated between running away screaming and throwing me into an imaginary jail. I did have to admit, this part I would miss.

Odd Job #17: Workout Novice

How I found the gig: Proposed the concept to my editor

Time worked: 10-15 hours per story

Pay: $75 per story

My abs hurt. My legs hurt. My body was covered in sweat. I may have been dying. I could not believe there were people who regularly did what I had just done.[41]

Hot yoga was invented by someone who clearly felt regular yoga wasn't painful and embarrassing enough, so they decided to hold their sessions in a room with a temperature somewhere between 90 and 100 degrees. The heat helps the body to stretch deeper than it normally can and to sweat out toxins. Because health nuts are terrified of toxins the way everyone else is terrified of Iran getting the bomb.

I had found a yoga studio in South Boston with countless five-star Yelp ratings. It was a credential that seemed positive until you actually read the reviews. "After a session with David you will be drenched in

---

[41] When I proposed that I write a recurring column about my experiences trying out different exercise fads, my editor asked me to submit a sample story. What follows is that submission, a piece about the time I tried hot yoga.

sweat and sore in places you didn't know existed," one proclaimed. *Awesome! I can't wait!*

When I arrived at the yoga studio, the air was so hot and thick I had to physically push through it. I was sweating within seconds. Even more upsetting, I was instantly aware of one unavoidable fact: Almost everyone there was a lot more attractive than I was.

The girls all had tight clothes hugging their tighter bodies. And I think most of them were wearing makeup. Which seemed like a horrendous choice for a workout guaranteeing intense perspiration, but what did I know?

There were only two men in the room besides me. One looked like he was using this session to kill time between trainings for the US Olympic gymnastics team, and the other was a balding man in his 40s wearing a knee brace. Deciding it would be best not to be in the immediate sightline of these gorgeous women during a class in which I would almost certainly look like a complete idiot, I sat down next to the balding 40-year-old. I also figured if anyone did glance my way, he would give me the best shot at looking competent by comparison. However, it soon became clear that there was no option that made me look competent by comparison. Knee Brace Guy ran circles around me.

Then our teacher entered, immediately apologizing to the room, "Sorry everyone, there's something wrong with the thermostat, but we think we've got the problem fixed." I breathed a sigh of relief. The place was supposed to be hot, but I was glad to learn it wouldn't be *this* hot.

She continued, "The heat should be turned up momentarily." I hated her already.

As the temperature climbed, we "eased into things" by gently leaning back on our calves. It was the first pose. The "we'll start off slow" pose. And already I was in pain. My knees hurt, and my legs began to cramp. This was going to suck.

Then everyone let loose a solid "Oooohhhmmm," which I had thought was only done by people making fun of meditation. I joined in the Oooohhhmmming, grateful for an area where I was as skilled as my classmates.

Over the next 40 minutes, we stretched and contorted our bodies in a fashion that I had previously thought we were protected from by the Eighth Amendment's prohibition against cruel and unusual punishment. In one pose, we grabbed our leg and lifted it into the air behind us while extending our body forward. In another, we turned into a stretch after wrapping our legs around each other the way you tie two shoelaces together.

Things got worse when we were instructed to elevate one foot into the air, loop a strap around it, and pull. That's right, hot yoga has a strap you wrap around your limbs and pull to stretch yourself further. Because when nature tells your body, "Hey, maybe you shouldn't stretch this part too much," the only reasonable response is to crank up the heat to loosen your muscles, then loop a strap around yourself and yank harder.

My abs spasmed uncontrollably. I tried in vain to wipe the sweat away, but it was like toweling off in the middle of a rainstorm. At one point, the instructor came over and reached out her arm to readjust my leg, but, presumably realizing how soaked I was, thought better of it and went with the more hands-off verbal instruction of "lift your foot a bit higher," then proceeded not to come near me for the rest of the session.

Forty-five minutes in I considered leaving, but figured how bad could 15 more minutes be? This was based on the faulty assumption that class lasted an hour. It turned out that the standard hot yoga session is an hour and a half, because, I mean, of course it is.

The whole time, my teacher had an annoying habit of implying that we were almost finished when that was nowhere near true. Saying things like, "And we're almost done." Pause. "With this pose." Or, "Don't worry, this is the last time we're going to use the strap." Pause. "Well, actually we're going to do one more after, but then we're done." She chuckled at her mistake. I loathed her.

Slowly but surely, time passed, and we were almost done for real. We went back to the painful starting pose or something close to it. Apparently, the instructor viewed this as a peaceful calm-down from the workout, but my body disagreed. I was ready for it all to be over. The heat. The physical pain. I've seen the yoga scenes in movies. I knew how this ended. With us saying "Namaste." *Just get to Namaste.*

She told us to imagine our body filling with blue light. As my thighs screamed out, she explained how we should share our light with the world. The soles of my feet were hurting. Who hurts the soles of their feet stretching? She said we should let our light wash over whomever we met, but I had a good idea of where she could shove her light. *Just get to Namaste.*

Then, one more time we were chanting "Ooooohhhhhmmm," until finally there came the sweet relief of Namaste.

Odd Job #18: Conjoined Twin

How I found the gig: Hired by a former client

Time worked: 6 hours

Pay: $250

My friend Carol and I were standing in the middle of a convention center, the two of us squeezed into one jumbo-sized T-shirt, playing the role of conjoined twins for the amusement of the passersby.

At this point I didn't find these gigs strange. They were normal. You want to pay me to be the freak in a weird costume and joke around with strangers? No problem. Truth be told, I enjoyed it. It was like making work a game. Do something interesting and goofy, and, at the end of the day, we'll pay you money.

And the folks I worked these gigs with were mostly fun people who wanted to earn their living doing fun things. In other words, they were the kind of people you could enjoy being trapped in a T-shirt with—and who jumped at the opportunity when you texted and said, "Hey, wanna be a conjoined twin with me for the day for $250?" For me, this was just another Friday working closely with a colleague.

John—the man who employed me for my bikini stunt and the "Workout Novice" pieces—had solicited my services again, this time to help promote his other business, an organization called Mediashower, by being the entertainment for his booth at a convention.

His hope was that attendees would be so struck by the two of us that they would have to stop and chat, at which point he would swoop in to discuss the benefits of working with his company.

Most businesses hire hot women in short shorts to achieve this goal. John had hired this:

The convention was centered around something called WordPress, which was the most commonly used web-design platform in the world, and Mediashower was taking this opportunity to unveil a new software product it had created that would work on any WordPress-built site.

I represented Mediashower, and Carol represented WordPress. The fact that we were bound together was supposed to symbolize how seamlessly the two of them integrated. Which was ironic, because seeing the two of us squeezed into a jumbo-sized T-shirt did not exactly bring to mind the phrase "seamless integration."[42]

Our outfit looked like it had been designed by a fourth grader for an art project that would soon be receiving a disappointing grade. The edges of the shirt buckled with each step we took while feathers shed everywhere, leaving a trail behind us that looked like something from a molting ostrich.

In retrospect, I'm not sure exactly what we were going for with the costume. I know the boa was meant to cover up the neck hole in the shirt so you couldn't see that we had two separate bodies. I think the hats were there to give the ensemble a sort of unifying theme. And the sunglasses were... well... I don't know what we were thinking with those. I believe they were supposed to help us stand out from the crowd, which, looking back, probably was not a concern.

It wasn't quite the look I pictured when we first took the assignment. Though even if we had known what we were getting into, Carol and I wouldn't have turned down the gig. After all, we were professional

---

[42] If you were to rank the phrases we brought to mind, it would probably go something like this: 1) I didn't realize they made shirts that large. 2) This has to be offensive to actual conjoined twins. 3) Wait, why is there a boa? 8) I thought a man and a woman couldn't be conjoined twins. 964) Seamless integration.

actors.[43]

As we stumbled into the convention on a Friday afternoon, I was struck by how gloomy the event felt. People shuffled aimlessly from booth to booth, more out of obligation than interest. Meanwhile, the vendors stared off into space, fingering their company-themed mouse pad giveaways that no one was taking, presumably because it wasn't 1997.

The whole room had a drabness that did not jibe especially well with the two zany characters at the corner booth in an XXXL T-shirt. I braced myself for snickers, uncomfortable glances, and an afternoon full of people hurrying past us, frightened we might try to talk to them.

But we weren't frightening. We were stars.

Convention attendees smiled, screamed, whipped out cameras, posed for pictures, and ate up our corny jokes. For John's part, he not only had the busiest booth, but he also had people snapping photos of us wearing his company logo and uploading those shots to Facebook, Instagram, and six more sites that I would know the names of if I was at all hip.

John smiled at the swarm of customers, and Carol and I got lost in the joy that is improv. We joked and bantered like a brother and sister who had been attached at the hip for decades. In return, the people there overlooked our flawed costume and the genetic impossibility we presented. Well, most people did.

"I told my friend that you're really Siamese twins," a woman whispered to us late in the day, snickering as she spoke. "And she believed me."

I was curious who her friend was, but we had a role to play. It was

---

[43] As always, "professional actors" can also be defined as "broke."

sort of like when you go to Colonial Williamsburg and you see some snotty guest say to the actor, "Man, it was tough getting here in our CAR." And then the actor has to do everything he can not to shoot himself before saying, "A car? What manner of wizardry is that?"

"We *are* twins," Carol said, doing her part.

"And we prefer the term 'conjoined,'" I said, doing mine.

"What?" The woman took a step back. "Wait, really? Oh my—I, I— oh. I had no idea."

You can't be falling for this.

"Show her the picture," Carol interjected.

The night before, Carol had found a picture of two kids online and taped our heads on top of them. The results were mildly mortifying.

"This is from when we were five," I explained, presenting the doctored image.

I figured the heads of two people, decades past age five and clearly taped onto children's bodies, would clarify the fact that we were kidding. But for her, this was not so much the punchline to a bad joke as it was proof.

"Oh my God, I have to go tell my friend," the woman announced. And she scampered off.

Carol and I looked at each other, slightly more concerned for the future of humanity than we had been before, then returned to our work.

It was Friday, and today we were conjoined twins.

Odd Job #19: Engineer

How I found the gig: Facebook

Time worked: 2 hours

Pay: I lost $70

Normally when it comes to building stuff, I am not someone you would call handy. Or someone you would call competent. Or really someone you would call at all. This is unfortunate, because no matter how much people like me tell ourselves that we have other strengths, and it's okay that we aren't the kind of real men who know how to make stuff with our hands, we know deep down inside that this means we are failures. But this summer, I had a chance to change that.

In Boston, the temperature had reached a level weathermen were describing as "Don't ever leave your hou—" before melting into a puddle on the sidewalk. It was perpetually over 90 degrees, and all those annoying people who like to complain, "It's not the heat, it's the humidity," had plenty to crow about.[44]

That meant my air conditioner was constantly running, and my

---

[44] I've said it before, I'll say it again: "Shut up. It's both."

electric bill was higher than the mercury in my thermometer. As I dragged my body into the apartment one day, fantasizing about living anywhere colder than Boston (a dream rarely articulated by anyone), I remembered an article a friend had linked to on Facebook explaining how to build a homemade A/C unit. The headline read, "I Couldn't Believe It, This Actually Works." Since internet headlines like that have never let me down, I scrolled through my bookmarks until I found the original piece and printed it out.

I was going to solve my heat problem, prove my manhood bona fides, and take a hatchet to my utility bill in one fell swoop.

I was going to make my own air conditioner.

Walking into the hardware store, I felt instantly lost and overwhelmed. My printout of the online instructions told me to get things with names like "PVC pipe" and "hole saw," which left me with unanswered follow-up questions like, "What the hell is a hole saw?"

Luckily, one of the sales clerks in the store was an old high school friend who kindly offered his assistance. He handed me items off the shelf while a cash register in my brain tallied the rising cost of this supposedly money-saving contraption.

"This says you need a lining for the bucket," he said to me. "How sturdy do you need it?"

I stared at him with the dumbfounded look of a five-year-old trying to solve an astrophysics problem. He nodded in a way that seemed to say, "My bad, I forgot you were totally useless. Don't worry, we'll get through this."

"Hey, Dalton," he called to his co-worker as he walked by. "You built a makeshift A/C unit once, right?"

"Yeah, why?" Dalton walked over as he spoke.

"Jon here is building one, and I'm wondering how rigid the liner needs to be." My friend held up the liner he had been planning to give me.

"Well, you want something with a bit more space than that, right?" Dalton asked me.

I gave Dalton my astrophysics look. But he wasn't as quick to accept my ignorance. "Essentially, there needs to be some space to allow the molecules to move around, right?" he asked. Dalton spoke like he was trying to establish the simple concepts before using them to explain more advanced ones, but it wasn't working. The foundational basics alone were too much for me.

"I'm really not sure," I told him.

"Here, follow me." Then Dalton and I were walking through the store as he pointed to different objects and said things like, "Molecules!" "Formulas!" "Physics!" I looked back longingly at my friend, but he was already helping someone else.

By the time we got to the checkout lane, Dalton had a new plan, and I was too out of my element to object. We were going to scrap the method I had found online and build something he assured me was "simpler."

He sketched out his vision on some scrap paper. It went like this: You fill a five-gallon bucket with ice. You cut a hole in the lid of the bucket and stick a fan in that hole. You then cut a hole in the side of the bucket and shove a hose through it. You turn on the fan, which recirculates the cool air coming off the ice, which flows through the hose and out into your room.

Molecules. Formulas. Physics.

"Okay," I said hesitantly.

I sat in my living room, staring at $70 worth of tools (goggles, drill, hole saw, X-Acto knife) and materials (bucket, hose, lid, ice), stuck with one frustrating problem: The end of the drill wasn't fitting into the hole saw the way it was supposed to. ~~It was eerily reminiscent of my prom night.~~

The hole saw is a cylinder, one end of which is sharp, and the other dull. You attach the dull end to a drill, and the drill's rapid rotation turns the sharp end into the perfect tool for carving a hole into something. In this case, I would be carving one in the side of the bucket to slide the hose through. My problem was that attaching the dull end to the drill was harder than I had expected.

Ten minutes of angrily leafing through the instruction manual had left me with a diagram of something that looked similar to what I wanted to do with a heading labeled "Removing the chuck." If you're thinking, "What's a chuck?" then you, like me, were not the manual's target audience.

The following is a direct quote from step two of this process. (Step one was unplugging the drill so you didn't disfigure your hand during step two. Step one was much more my speed.)

> Insert a 5/16" or larger hex key into the chuck and tighten the chuck jaws securely. Make sure each of the chuck jaws is seated on the flat surfaces of the hex key.

I'm sure that to whoever wrote this—a guy that presumably used phrases like "hex keys" and "chuck jaws" in casual conversation—these instructions were crystal clear. However, for someone like me, nothing short of the Rosetta Stone was getting me to step three.

It took 30 minutes before I finally got the saw to lock into place, though I'm still not sure how I did it. I put on my eyewear, turned on the drill, and slowly bore a hole into the bucket. And as the saw sliced through the plastic, something unexpected happened: The thing in front of me started taking on the exact shape illustrated on the sheet of paper. I was doing this.

I raced through each step of the process. I massaged the hose through the carved-out hole in the side of the bucket. Then I sliced a perfect hole in the lid for the fan. I fashioned a hood out of cardboard that I could put around the hose inside the bucket to funnel the cold air. And if you don't understand that last sentence, it's because I'm a man who knows how to build things, and you're a loser! Bam!

By the time I was done, I was surrounded by shavings from the skewered bucket while my goggles rested peacefully on my head. Waves of adrenaline surged through me as I stared at the thing that I had made with my own two hands.

I hurriedly emptied the bags of ice into the bucket and stuck it in the

corner of the room. I threw the fan on top, hit the on switch and…
It worked!
Cold air poured out of the hose.
For about five minutes, I was on top of the world. I was freakin' Thomas Edison.
Then, after a few moments of raging excitement, it was suddenly all over. ~~It was exactly like my prom night.~~

While freezing air poured out the hose, cooling the space immediately around the unit, the overall temperature of the room remained unaffected. I had essentially created a giant $70 ice cube.

Frustrated, I plopped down on my bed, confronted with the same two realities I faced when I began this project: I wasn't a man, and it was going to be a long, hot summer.

Odd Job #20: Bargain Hunter

How I found the gig: My mom

Time worked: 2 hours

Pay: Impossible to calculate

I was not very religious growing up. I attended a Jewish day school, but my parents sent me there more for the good teachers it employed than for any religious reasons. During the High Holidays, we'd put in a couple of appearances at synagogue, but we did it the way people show up for a few hours at the company Christmas party, because they want the boss to feel like they care.

Most religious edicts we ignored. Especially the one about attending services on Saturday mornings. Saturday was the day my mother and sister attended garage sales. And it was those garage sales that got the dogmatic devotion most families reserve for their faith.

When the weather got nice, my sister—who was a threat to commit manslaughter if anyone tried to wake her before noon most other weekend mornings—would get up early,[45] throw down breakfast, and

---

[45] By which I mean teenager-on-a-weekend early. So, you know, 9:30.

head out with my mom in search of the best bargains. They would come home laughing and smiling, showing off all the delightful things they had bought for only a few dollars.

I asked if I could come with them one time, and they obliged. But ten minutes into our trip, I realized that this was a disguised version of my most hated childhood activity: clothes shopping. After that, I stayed home. But I was still the beneficiary of their work. I would get toys and books and games that I enjoyed as much as if they were brand new.

Sometimes, my mother would speak wistfully of the perfect garage sale conditions, doing so with the air of a lovesick teenager imagining a date with one of the popular boys. She dreamed about a sale hosted by an upper-class family. One featuring handcrafted furniture, elegant clothes, and brand-name housewares all at discount prices. But unfortunately, rich people—whether it's because they don't need the money or because they're worried how it would look to peddle their used goods on the sidewalk—usually just throw their old things out or, even more upsetting to the garage sale community, donate everything to charity.

So she and my sister shopped in the upper-middle-class neighborhoods, which were the best one could hope for. Except one day of the year, when the circumstances collided to create the bargain hunter's perfect storm: The Gooding School Yard Sale. If garage sales were the religion of our family, then the Gooding School Yard Sale was its Christmas.

The Gooding School was a private school in a ritzy neighborhood with an annual tuition that was more than most people spent on a new car. While this, combined with generous alumni donations, meant that their hosting a rummage sale to raise money was kind of like Google hosting a car wash to cover the cost of some long-overdue office repairs, no one in my family was about to object. The Gooding School Yard Sale finally gave rich people a motivation to sell their stuff: the need to one-up the other parents.

When I heard that this annual event was approaching, I decided it might finally be time to embrace my family heritage. The *Odd Jobs* blog had gotten me hooked on money-saving opportunities, and suddenly one of the biggest ones in the city was almost upon us.

Perhaps the better religious metaphor for the Gooding School Yard Sale would be Mecca. The destination at the end of a pilgrimage that thousands make every year. We arrived ten minutes before the scheduled 9 a.m. kickoff time to find an army of attendees waiting outside in a line that curled around the school's entire soccer field. It was like the Wal-Mart crowd on Black Friday, only without that whole fear of getting knifed by someone who would rather have a death on his hands than miss out on a discount blender.

The doors opened, and everyone shuffled into the school gymnasium-turned-flea market filled wall-to-wall with people's old junk. My first instinct: I want it all.

I need bowls for the apartment! And chairs! Is that a treadmill?! I want that lovely bread box despite the fact that it's far too nice to go with anything in our kitchen. And I never have bread. That page-a-day calendar looks whimsical even though no one uses page-a-day calendars anymore and it's from 2011.

I told myself to calm down. To not grab anything for at least a few minutes while I got my sea legs. And as I did, my trip to a rummage sale slowly transformed into a visit to the zoo. A chance to watch bargain hunters in their natural habitat. There were the savvy pros, who cared nothing for the lives of the people they barreled over on their way to unbeatable prices. There were the volunteers who viewed this as a chance to chit-chat with the other parents. And then there were the suburban fathers who wore a look on their faces that could best be described as "I don't want to be here, but Barbara made me come in case she decided to get a dresser and needed help carrying it to the car."

My field studies were interrupted by a booming voice over the loud speaker. "We are missing a young girl named Lindsay… Lindsay, your mother has lost you. Please come to the toy department to meet your mother." As the announcement carried across the room, you could feel the parents judging the mom who had chosen discount goods over family while at the same time realizing that if that casserole dish over there had been $5 cheaper, they probably would have done the same thing.

My eyes eventually settled on my first purchase: a decades-old Mark McGwire lunchbox. There was something about the idea of a kid's lunchbox—the ultimate sign of hero worship—being adorned with the image of one of sports' now most-disgraced athletes that tickled me.

"How much is this?" I asked a volunteer.

She looked at it, "Ummm… $2?"

"You just made that number up right now, didn't you?"

"Yeah. Is that too steep?"

I felt guilty calling $2 steep and guiltier still haggling over the price at a fundraiser, but... yeah, for a used Mark McGwire lunchbox, it felt a little steep. But I made no waves and handed her the $2. Each of my purchases yielded the same conflicting feelings: that I had just scored a great deal and that I could have spent less. As I went along, I increased my haul. A dart board without darts, a set of mismatched Jenga blocks, a dingy chair and some exercise pants I didn't have a chance to try on, all for $12. Who ripped off whom in these deals? Impossible to tell.

But as I carried my bounty out the door, I felt a sort of dual joy. The happiness that comes from getting new toys along with the gratification that comes from leaving any shopping experience having dropped only $12. When I returned to my apartment, I proudly placed my purchases in their new home.

My family was right: That was more fun than going to synagogue.

The Want Ads

May 2014

Before I was broke, a dollar was a unit of currency so insignificant that I would spend it without hesitation. It was one-seventh of a bad sandwich from the place up the street. But when I started struggling to make ends meet, it morphed into something precious. Decisions to get an item as cheap as a candy bar weighed on me. Sometimes I would glance at the options near the register and tell myself I simply had to say no, it was too much. Other times I would find myself picking up a 3 Musketeers and marching slowly toward the cashier, all the while thinking, "I can't afford this."

So one of the best feelings I had in the time after online

poker folded came several years in, when I went out for drinks with a couple of friends one night. The restaurant was pricier than I was expecting, but when the server casually pointed at our empty glasses and asked, "Another round?" I said yes without thinking. And as we sat and joked about our days, I wasn't focused on how much I hated myself for spending more than I should have. I was focused on my friends and the fun we were having. I couldn't afford to ignore how much things cost every night, but it felt good to realize I could do so every now and then.

I had picked up a few more recurring gigs I enjoyed and started writing for a second website. In addition, looking for ways to save money that I could blog about had gotten me in the habit of reading personal finance websites, asking friends for money advice, and doing some thinking about my spending. Over the previous few years, the way I approached money had slowly morphed until one day it stopped feeling like the dollars always ran out too soon. I even could afford to do what was once unthinkable: turn down work.

Odd Jobs was about all the opportunities I took, but I didn't sign up for everything I saw. For example, a few times a month, I would see a fertility clinic listing on Craigslist that read "☆ ★ GOT SPERM? -- Earn up to $1,200/Month ★ ☆."[46] Making $1,200 a month generating sperm definitely fell under the heading of getting-rich-doing-what-you-love, and helping people who couldn't conceive seemed noble.[47] But the thought of

---

[46] You can tell it's legit because they used stars.

[47] Plus, imagine all the joy I would get from calling the sperm bank to schedule an appointment and saying such lines as, "I can't wait to come inside the clinic," "This sounds like a great opportunity because no matter how much money I have, I always end up blowing my load on my girlfriend," "I have an old car with no front-wheel drive, and I saw your facility is located on a steep

having offspring I would never meet was too difficult to bear. So I never did it.

Below are some more gigs I saw but never applied for. The original listing is in bold and included verbatim (though in some cases, parts of the original post have been cut for length reasons, and the names of the companies have been changed). My reactions follow in regular font and, of course, in the footnotes.

Pet Waste Removal Technician

Are you a reliable, hardworking, responsible person who loves working outdoors and likes dogs? Do you enjoy working independently? The Doo Doo Crew is a fast growing national pet waste removal company and we need help!

In case you needed any more proof that we've gone overboard fancying up people's job descriptions to make them feel good, look no further than the title "pet waste removal technician."

As a business model, this actually sounded interesting. The company's website (which of course declared "doody is our duty") explained that their staff would come to your house and clean up pet waste in all the places you didn't, like your

---

hill. If I can't get it up, are you going to be sympathetic and understanding, or will you berate me like that girl in college?" And, of course, "I know another sperm bank that's offering a better price, but if you can beat it for me, I'll go with you."

backyard.

But I had issues with the job description.

For example, is whether or not you like dogs truly relevant in this conversation? I like my friends, but that doesn't mean I want to pick up their intestinal waste. Hell, it sounded like when you arrived at a client's home, the dogs might not even be there. It would just be a one-on-one visit between you and their feces.

And the phrase "working independently" seemed like a stretch. Sure, you weren't sitting in a cubicle with a supervisor looking over your shoulder. But "independent" also implied a level of freedom to do what you want when you want that seemed to be inherently lacking in any position requiring you to drive over and clean up an animal's bowel movements every time someone called.

Female needed for Sexy Trivial Pursuit gig – $1000

I'm a mid 30s overworked finance professional living and working downtown with a fun gig to offer the right girl. I'm looking for a beautiful, refined, and fiercely intelligent girl to play Trivial Pursuit with, with cold hard cash as your prize ($1000). But we'll play with some twists on the rules to make things more interesting:

* if you miss your question, you have

> to either remove an article of clothing or down half a shot of your liquor of choice.
>
> * if you miss your question after you've run out of clothes, you have to either down half a shot or receive three bare-bottomed spanks.
>
> The game finishes the usual way, when you've filled up your pie piece[48] with all the colors and make it to the center of the board.[49]
>
> That's all there is to the gig. Good clean fun. Must be attractive and fit and send a clear picture with your reply.

I think it's safe to say that the ship sailed on "good clean fun" with the introduction of the phrase "three bare-bottomed spanks." And the ship absolutely sailed on getting a refined girl when you made it a prerequisite that applicants be interested in being your trivia sex slave for a thousand bucks.

But there was a bigger problem with this listing: You can't post something like this and NOT DISCLOSE WHICH TRIVIAL

---

[48] Please don't let "filled up your pie piece" be a euphemism. Please don't let "filled up your pie piece" be a euphemism.

[49] There are a lot of things about this job offer that upset me, but perhaps nothing more than the fact that this guy believed this is the normal way a Trivial Pursuit game ends. I mean, what kind of animal thinks that you simply have to make it to the middle but don't need to answer a question in the category of your opponent's choice when you get there?

PURSUIT GENUS YOU ARE USING. Because if it was one of the newer versions, then maybe signing up for this wouldn't be the worst decision in the world. But if this was one of those Trivial Pursuits from 1980, with geography questions that assume West Germany is still a thing (i.e. the version everyone inexplicably still has in their home today), then even the most intelligent women would end up naked within half an hour of arriving.

LOVE WORKING OUTSIDE – BE A VALET PARKER OPEN THE DOOR TO NEW HORIZONS

[Due to copyright laws, I have not included the picture that went with this ad. But it was a car door opening onto a majestic view of the ocean and skyline. Presumably these were the new horizons described in the headline.]

Spread your wings and come park with us...[50]

Click Here to Apply Online

ParkPlace is looking for valet parking attendants to join our team of parking professionals. We have positions

---

[50] "I'm so sick of this dead-end corporate world! I want to spread my wings and become a parking lot attendant!"
-No one ever

> available in both our Hotel (shift is 3:00pm-11:30pm) and Restaurant Division (shift is 5:00pm-12:00am). **Compensation is based upon business levels of the location assigned to you and range from $6-$10 per hour, PLUS tips!**

It takes a certain level of audacity to promote being a valet with the line "love working outside." Somehow, I have trouble picturing rugged whitewater-rafting enthusiasts scratching their outdoorsy itch parking cars. Also, I left out the text that told prospective employees that they would be stationed in the garage of a downtown Boston shopping mall, a place that definitely doesn't have majestic views of the water meeting the skyline.

Finally, let's take a moment to appreciate the word "PLUS" being in all caps, and the word "tips" coming with an exclamation point at the end of it. As if to say, "$6-$10 per hour alone is pretty amazing, but... YOU'LL EARN TIPS TOO!" Yeah, thanks for throwing those in, but I'd feel guilty taking extra money when you're already offering me a pay range whose bottom end leaves me below minimum wage.

Single girls job/personal assistant

> Hi! I'm gonna be blunt...I am a single guy, 33, live alone, i work a lot and I'm willing to pay...I need companionship and personal assistant combination...

> I don't discriminate but you must be a female[51]...chores: cleaning, laundry, some cooking, pampering me, taking care of my need. IM LOOKING FOR A WIFE WITH A AGREEMENT. JK no marriage just the responsibilities that a homemaker wife would have...email with responses. Looking forward to meeting you.

I'll give the guy this: Normally whenever someone says, "I'll be blunt," you can be pretty sure they're about to be anything but. But this man makes it as clear as he possibly can, while still avoiding getting banned by Craigslist's algorithms, that he's looking for a prostitute/butler combination. He says that applicants must be single women, he refers to taking care of his need (gross), and he uses the term "A WIFE WITH A AGREEMENT."[52] So even though he never mentions sex outright, by the time you reach the line "looking forward to meeting you," you have everything you need to know just how much you're not looking forward to meeting him.

Need Help Making a Quality Robot to Cyborg Aerial Strip Tease Costume

> I am performing an aerial piece for the extreme future fest and need a

---

[51] Discrimination.
[52] [*sic*]. A thousand times [*sic*].

> quality old school robot costume that I can both wear on the static trapeze and strip off to become a semi-nude, burlesque styled cyborg. I am looking for a quality costume. Need by Dec 1. Initial thoughts are to use 80's looking computer and electronic parts for the robot and attachable cyborg skin pieces and or body paint stencils for the cyborg part. Further creative ideas totally acceptable.

Actually, I have no jokes here. This person and the future fest both sound awesome.

I mean, don't get me wrong, doing semi-nude cyborg trapeze dancing doesn't offer quite the feeling of liberation you get parking cars or the feeling of independence that comes with cleaning up dog poop. But then again, what does?

Odd Job #21: Game Show Applicant

How I found the gig: Random cold call from someone who worked on the show

Time worked: 2 hours

Pay: $0

"Yeah, I was on *Who Wants to be a Millionaire?*" one man said to the woman next to him as I stood behind them, eavesdropping.

"We were both on *Jeopardy*," a couple in another part of the room related.

We were assembled in a waiting room, about to head into an audition for a game show I had never heard of called *The Dungeon*. It was apparently a trivia competition, though I didn't know why you would call a quiz show *The Dungeon*, nor did I know why the program's website featured a scary, muscular man covered in tattoos glaring back at me over a caption reading "CAN YOU HANDLE THE DUNGEON MASTER?"[53] But those two details made me a bit worried about what would happen if I got an answer wrong.

---

[53] My immediate instinct was that I could not.

The people around me discussed their game show experiences the way I talked about that time I played in the World Series of Poker: an event whose memory was permanently implanted in our brains with near photographic accuracy. Right down, of course, to the moment when we lost.

"I got the $8,000 question wrong," one of them explained, clearly still anguished about it four years later.

Another, with a nametag reading Donald, said, "They asked me who wrote *East of Eden*, and I went blank."

"John Steinbeck," said the person next to him, as though what Donald really wanted to hear was someone demonstrating how obvious the answer was.

"Yeah, I know," Donald said dejectedly. Of course he knew. Donald could suffer a traumatic brain injury and still never forget that John Steinbeck wrote *East of Eden*.

Half the people there were game show veterans, the rest simply loved *The Dungeon*. One superfan next to me had wanted to audition so badly that he took a bus in from Washington, DC. And the guy next to him was spending his wait time pontificating to the others about how the American version of the show compared to the original, which apparently aired in the Netherlands.[54] I was beginning to think I was the only one there simply because I had an afternoon to kill.

"All right!" I heard a voice call from the doorway. "If I could have everyone line up along this wall, we'll call you in one at a time to take your picture. After that, grab a seat and get ready for the exam."

---

[54] By his rigorous analysis, the shows were similar, "but the US host is hotter."

The exam, a series of 40 trivia questions of varying degrees of difficulty, was what would ultimately determine whether we qualified for the show. How the dungeon master played into all of this never came up.

As people churned through the line, the coordinator for the show chatted them up. "Where ya from? How'd you hear about this? You watch the show?" Each applicant talked for a minute or two, then was called over for the photo. Once the person left, I saw the coordinator jot down notes on a sheet of paper, presumably documenting his reactions. My general understanding is that, in addition to subject knowledge, these shows are looking for personalities. Contestants that people want to watch on TV. My hope was that this was where I would find my edge.

Because standing in the waiting area, I had discerned two things that, in a room full of people whose lives were devoted to memorizing useless facts, were probably not that surprising: One, everyone there was a lot smarter than me. And two, certain basics of human interaction seemed to elude most of them. I couldn't beat them on the trivia battlefield. But when I hosted trivia games at bars and restaurants, being fun and engaging was literally my job.

(You might point out that trivia was also my job, but I wasn't very good at that part.)

As a *Dungeon* staffer finished his spirited back and forth with the man ahead of me about something painfully nerdy, I tried to get my head right. *You got this. You're fun. You're cool. Everyone else here is an awkward, unkempt nerd. I think the person in front of you just spent his 30 seconds talking about who the best Star Trek captain was.*[55]

---

[55] I mean, obviously it's Jean-Luc Picard from *Next Generation,* but still, there's a time and a place.

"How you doing?" the employee asked.

"Good, how are you?" I answered. *I am crushing this.*

"Doing good." Then there was silence. *Wait, what happened? Where is my witty banter? Where are the questions you asked everyone else?*

"So... How'd you hear about us?" He sounded like he was struggling to fill the silence. *No! I'm the charming one! Don't you know this is my edge??*

"Actually, I host trivia games at bars and restaurants, and somebody from your organization was just randomly calling different places that run trivia events and asking the hosts to mention these auditions to their players. And when he talked to me, I was like, 'I wanna try out!'"

Then he stared at me, unsure what to say next. *Come on! That anecdote gives you so much to work with.*

"Jonathan," the photographer called me over. I no longer had faith in my edge.

The opening question was a gimme. *21 Jump Street*. I put down the answer, but told myself not to get cocky. The first one was always easy.

"What is the only South American country whose name starts with the letter E?" *Shoot, I know this. Right? I should know this. I'm sure it's obvious. I'm going to look this up later and hate myself, aren't I?*[56]

The questions after that varied in difficulty. Ranging from the easy ("Who plays the boss on the American version of *The Office*?") to the

---

[56] Yup. It's Ecuador.

medium ("Which president is known as the Father of the Constitution?") to the thank-god-this-came-up-at-my-job-last-week-otherwise-I-would-not-have-gotten-it ("What was the name of John Wilkes Booth's brother, who saved Abraham Lincoln's son's life only months before President Lincoln was assassinated?") to the are-you-kidding-me ("What is the best-selling variety of cabbage in the United States?")[57]

Here and there I got a few right, but by the time I passed in my sheet, it was full of wrong guesses and stars that I used as reminders to "come back to this one" alongside questions I never returned to.

The staffers took our quizzes out into the hallway, and immediately the room broke into a post-mortem.

"Yeah what was that one?" said a man on my left. "I knew it was either [mumbled word I couldn't make out] or [mumbled word I couldn't make out]."

"Right, I narrowed it down to those two, too," said another.

"It was [mumbled word I couldn't make out]," answered a third one confidently.

"Yeah, that's what I thought," said the first.

"Which one are you talking about?" I interjected. I might not get on TV, but maybe I could have my moment by knowing at least one answer in front of these people.

"The cabbage question," answered the first guy. *Seriously? They narrowed down the freaking cabbage question to one of two options?*

"I'm telling you," said someone else, "it's [word which was not mumbled but still sounded like gibberish since it's a type of cabbage, and

---

[57] Frankly, it was news to me that there even were multiple varieties of cabbage out there.

how does anybody know different types of cabbage?]."

I was done with these people.

Sitting on the other side of me was Donald, he of the failed *East of Eden* question. When I turned to him, he either didn't know the cabbage answer or at least had the decency not to bring it up. We commiserated over the ones that we knew deep down inside but just couldn't get. He told me that the one on the tip of my tongue was "Jack Ruby." I could not begin to tell him the one on the tip of his.

"Some of them I thought were a good, solid difficulty," I said. "Like the Edwin Booth question." The question didn't mention Edwin Booth, it just asked for Lincoln's assassin's brother's name. But I wanted Donald to ask, "Which one was that?" Then I could say, "Oh, you didn't get that one? Sorry, I meant the question that asked for the name of John Wilkes Booth's brother. It was Edwin Booth." Was this petty? Sure. But I needed a win at that moment.

"Yeah, the Edwin Booth question?" Donald said, not following the script I had mentally assigned him. "That one was pretty obvious." I was now done with this guy, too.

The staff returned to the room and began reading off the list of people they wanted to stick around. With each non-Jonathan name, I became a little more pessimistic. They reached the end, and it was clear I had been eliminated.

Then I was leaving the room and heading home. The cute girl who checked us in smiled at me as I left, and I felt mildly better. I tried to flirt with her, but I could tell that only made her regret smiling at me, so I stopped. I no longer felt mildly better.

I walked down the stairs and out the exit.

I was not surprised. I had made peace with my trivia deficiencies long ago. But it would have been nice to get to round two.

"Excuse me," a tourist with a foreign accent said as I headed up the street. "Do you know how to get downtown from here?"

Even the threat of an about-to-expire parking meter couldn't stop me from turning to him, smiling, and giving directions. It felt good to know something that someone else didn't.

Odd Job #22: Rock Star

How I found the gig: TaskRabbit

Time worked: 4 hours (prep time) + 10 minutes (the performance)

Pay: $55

I couldn't tell whether Racquel was the coolest girlfriend in the world or the worst. These things are tough to determine when someone gives a gift that is both perfectly sappy and relentlessly embarrassing. You know, like when a guy has an eight-foot-tall teddy bear and giant bouquet of flowers delivered to his girlfriend's office where everyone will see them.

For her part, Racquel was looking for a singer to serenade her beau with a boy-band song in a very public venue at 8 a.m. on Valentine's Day.

The coolest girlfriend in the world or the worst? I'm not sure.

"Charlie," Racquel explained over the phone, "is a huge One Direction fan." For future generations who read this and don't know the band One Direction, they were five young and attractive guys who, in the early 2010s, collectively spent what had to have been 50 hours a week styling their hair, then ten more cranking out generic songs with auto-tuned voices that seemed to double as mating calls for 13-year-old girls.

In other words, it makes total sense that Charlie was single when Racquel met him.

"I want to surprise him with someone doing a silly version of the song 'Kiss You,'" she continued. I assumed she meant someone doing a silly version of the song *in person*. Because the mission of doing a silly version of "Kiss You" had already been accomplished by One Direction themselves and uploaded to the World Wide Web.[58] It is the kind of video that seamlessly blends guys rubbing each other's nipples with guys doing the Macarena while skiing with guys doing prison dance numbers in some of the most fashionable inmate clothes you have ever seen. It is the kind of video that you hope isn't the only example future archeologists will find of our society's accomplishments.

"There's a parking lot a few minutes from Charlie's dorm," she explained. I would be coming by car since I had volunteered the use of my sound system for this project. "If you can get there ten minutes early, that would be perfect."

"I'm sorry, did you say dorm?" I asked.

"Yeah, we're students at Harvard."

"Which means we're doing this in his dorm room?" I hoped my phone was having reception problems and that what she'd really said was, "There's a parking lot a few minutes from Charlie's norm…al residence, which is a private home located in the middle of the woods."

"No," she said. *Oh, thank God.* "I'm picturing you'll be outside on the quad with the speakers projecting your voice up to his room." *Never mind.*

"Doesn't that mean we might be waking kids up at 8 a.m. with the sound of me belting out One Direction?" I was beginning to regret having

---

[58] http://www.youtube.com/watch?v=T4cdfRohhcg

offered to bring speakers.

"I don't think anyone will mind getting up that early," she said, thereby proving that she had never met a single college student in her life.

Before we ended the call, we covered a few last details, like what dance moves I planned to use ("The more sexually suggestive, the better," she told me) and some ways I could alter the lyrics to include references to their relationship. (Apparently there was an incident where he had accidentally kicked her in her lady parts that she wanted me to include. Clearly, Charlie and Racquel had built something special in their time together.)

I spent the next week locked in my room, singing the song again and again. I pored over the words, looking for places to artfully plug in casual references to Charlie kicking his girlfriend in the nether regions. And, of course, perfecting my dance moves.

When Valentine's Day finally arrived, I was ready.

"Charlie ended up spending the night at my apartment," Racquel told me when we met up the morning of the big day. "Which, unfortunately, means you'll have to sing the song there and not in front of the entire dorm."

I nodded, marveling at how different our definitions of the word *"unfortunately"* were. "I'm sorry to hear that," I lied.

"Also, I told him you were a friend visiting from Chicago. Just to warn you, he's a little sketched out that I've been acting evasive and now I'm meeting up with some guy at 7:30 in the morning, then bringing him to our apartment on Valentine's Day." *Oh good. I was worried this would be uncomfortable.*

"No problem."

When we arrived, Charlie was waiting on the couch, clearly annoyed.

"This is my friend from Chicago," she told him.

"Don't have much luggage," he said, nodding at my sound system.

Ha, yes, well, you know, I uh, I mean I uh—"I travel light," I said. He nodded skeptically. "I'm sorry to do this, but do you mind if I check something with my speakers? I'm worried one of them might be broken, and my band has a show tonight."

Charlie gave me a look that seemed to say, "Why the hell not? You're already making yourself at home in every other way possible." I took this as him granting approval and began setting up.

I could feel my hands shaking as I plugged in my equipment. I tried some deep breathing to calm myself, but it was useless. Acting over the years had taught me that this would happen sometimes. I knew that once I got going, the nerves would disappear. But until then, there was nothing I could do.

I finished getting things ready, took one last deep breath, then flipped on the mic.

"Charlie," I said, turning to face him and Racquel. "You've probably figured out that I'm not visiting from out of town. I'm here as a special guest at Racquel's request. She knows how much you love One Direction, and she asked the band if they could perform for you today. They said they couldn't be here, but they asked me to come in their place.

So this is for you."

I pressed play on the song as the opening chords started in the background. I could feel the butterflies disappearing as I slowly stopped being me and became the sixth member of One Direction. "Oh, I just wanna take you anywhere that you like," I shouted into my microphone as the music kicked up a notch.

Did I mention that I'm a terrible singer? Like really terrible? The kind who clears the dance floor when he sings karaoke, then, when he gets back to his friends, hears one of them say, "Good for you. Most people who can't sing are usually totally inhibited up there."

I had warned Racquel about these limitations, but I'm guessing Charlie wasn't expecting my voice to sound quite so much like a beached whale. "Baby, I'll take you there, take you there. Baby, I'll take you there, yeah," I bellowed, the music flowing through me.

I glanced at Charlie to see if he had softened at all. Or if he had any feelings about this man in his girlfriend's living room offering to take him there, take him there, yeah. But he wasn't Charlie the grouch any more. He was Charlie the fan boy. A giant smile had spread across his face, and he and his girlfriend were bobbing up and down to the music.

My voice got better, sounding more like actual singing. Or at least, that's what I told myself as the two of them and I got lost in the moment. "Oh tell me tell me tell me how to turn your love on. Is it by singing One di-re-eh-ehc-shon?" I said, throwing in my first deviation from the actual song. It was, admittedly, a bit uninspired.

"Baby just shout it out, shout it out, like a kid at God ca-a-a-mp, yeah." (Apparently, Charlie went to religious camp as a child. Something Racquel had been teasing him about for years and now wanted a stranger to sing about in his living room. Again, coolest girlfriend or worst girlfriend? Who can say?)[59]

"And if yoo-ooo-ooo, you want me too-ooo-ooo," I pointed suggestively at Charlie as I held my ooo's and flashed a flirtatious smile, "let's make a moo-oove."

And then came the chorus. The dance moves flew into high gear. Pelvic thrusts at moments not totally justified. Long, sexy stares into Racquel's and Charlie's eyes. And running of fingers down my body when describing the kind of ru-uh-ush I get every time we tou-uh-uch.

But I also pulled out some of the boy band classics. There was jumping up and down, bending all the way to the floor as I held notes, and that one where you hold the mic to the audience during the "yeah yeah yeah"s so they'll sing along.[60]

As I performed, I became a rock star. The two of them went wild. They danced and jumped and sang right along with me. It was as though I was the actual band and they were my rabid fans.

When I finished the song and took my bows, Racquel rushed over to thank me, clapping excitedly. I smiled, she slid me a tip, we enjoyed the moment and then...

It got awkward.

---

[59] If you're curious about how the crotch-kicking line got worked in, I changed the words from the original, "Oh I just wanna show you off to all of my friends/ making them drool down their chinny-chin-chins" to "Oh I just wanna kick you where the sun don't shine/ like you did to Racquel that one time." The line wasn't great, but considering it was replacing "making them drool down their chinny-chin-chins," which was apparently supposed to rhyme with the word "friends" on a track certified Gold by the RIAA, it's tough to feel too bad about my lyrics.

[60] It should be noted that "Kiss You" is 60 percent "yeah yeah yeah"s.

After all, what is there to say to a couple of strangers that you just debased yourself in front of for their pleasure? Packing up my sound system, I felt like the stripper picking her clothes off the floor at a bachelor party after the show was over.

Then we said our goodbyes, and I shuffled out the door.

I'll always be a bit curious what the next five minutes were like. Was Charlie happy with his gift? Embarrassed? Would his reaction have been different if we had done it on the quad, my speakers waking up half the campus as my voice carried to his window? What was his answer to the Racquel question? Was she the coolest girlfriend in the world or the worst?

I guess, maybe, she could have been both.

Odd Job #23: Substitute Teacher

How I found the gig: Referred by a friend

Time worked: 7 hours

Pay: $70

Usually, word would start to spread around second period. "Mrs. Nelson isn't here today."

"She's not?"

In high school, there was no greater thrill than having a substitute teacher.

"Yeah. I think her brother died."

"Oh my God. That's amazing."

The poor sub never had a chance. Half the students would cut class, and the other half would pretend they were someone they weren't during attendance, as, you'll have to take my word for it, this was the most hilarious prank in the world. As the period went on, the room would turn into a gymnasium, the noise level would escalate past that of a

Boeing 747, and the substitute would frantically try to get ahold of his therapist for an emergency session. In our eyes, the fill-ins were never really human. They were more like the guy in the picture clipped to the clothesline at the shooting range.

So when my friend, a teacher in a school district 30 minutes outside of Boston, proposed that I be a substitute where he worked, sirens went off in my head.

"Well, I don't have a teaching degree," I told him, fumbling for an excuse.

"Doesn't matter," he said, shrugging. "I think they just want someone with a pulse."

It was good to see that the standards for being a sub hadn't changed since I graduated.

"How much does it pay?" I asked.

"Something like $70 a day."

"What time would I have to be there?"

"Probably 7 a.m."

No wonder they never got the most qualified individuals.

It was bizarre walking through the halls of Willis Middle School, watching students bustle to and from their lockers around me. My only experience with this ecosystem was as a member of its population. I had only ever been that kid running to class or that one talking loudly to a friend about the upcoming weekend. That person for whom there was no bigger villain than the Earth Science teacher and no bigger dream than getting a date with Becky Summers in English. I had never been the spectator able to step back and observe how inconsequential these seemingly all-important things actually were. I suppose decades from now, this is how I will look back at the things I think of as problems in my life today.

"Here ya go," Ms. Jennings said as she turned on the lights in the classroom where I would be filling in for the health teacher. "Now if any of these kids gives you a hard time, let me know. I'll take care of them." It was the second time one of the teachers had told me to let her know if the students gave me a hard time and subsequently offered to "take care of them." One person saying it would have been comforting. Two people saying it had the opposite effect.

Ms. Jennings left, and I familiarized myself with the room. I noticed that the curriculum for health had not changed much in the last 15 years: Namely, everything fun will ruin your life. I saw a diagram breaking down all the bad things that could happen if you smoked pot next to a diagram of what could happen if you drank alcohol next to a diagram of what could happen if you did crystal meth. Because marijuana, alcohol, crystal meth, those things are equal.

A poster on the wall showed a teenager who couldn't go out with her friends because she had to take care of her if-only-I-had-used-a-fucking-condom child. "Going out doesn't mean going all the way. Going all the way might mean you can't go out," it read. I smiled. It was clever. Not clever enough to trump the appeal of sex to a teenager whose hormones were going berserk, but still clever.

"Hi, are you the sub?" I heard a voice ask from behind me. I turned around to face another teacher. "I'm Ms. Harrington. My classroom is right next door. I just wanted to introduce myself and say that if any of the kids gives you a hard time, let me know. I'll take care of them." *What the hell are these children doing to their subs? And why does everyone seem to have such a lust for "taking care of them"?* I thanked her, and she left.

I leafed through the lesson plan I had received. The first class would be watching a VHS tape from the Red Cross on CPR, so I'm guessing the school's health department was having some financial struggles. It may have, in fact, been the same cassette I had to watch back when I was in seventh grade. The next class would be doing a rigorous set of worksheets that had something to do with self-esteem. But it was third period with the eighth graders that caught my eye. Two other teachers and I would be assisting Ms. Norton as she taught a class on sexuality. Because if there's one thing kids like more than talking to an adult about bumping uglies, it's talking to a group of adults about it.

I breezed through the first two classes, delighted to discover that I did not need to contact any teachers to "take care of" anyone. Soon enough it was third period, and Ms. Norton, the sex-ed teacher, was walking into the room.

There is always something unsettling about professional sex-ed teachers. Their goal is to make students comfortable, to help them understand that they don't have to be embarrassed to talk with an adult about sexuality. But as these instructors speak nonchalantly and act like the cool aunt or uncle, they come off as a little too eager to talk to someone 30 years their junior about doing the funky funk.

Call me old-fashioned, but I prefer someone like my seventh-grade gym teacher, who taught us with the disposition of a man trying to avoid a lawsuit with every word he spoke. Who spent most of the time shaking, sweating, and avoiding eye contact as he bumbled through words like "erection" and "vagina." Now that's what a sex-ed teacher should look like.

"I'm a nurse in the high school," Ms. Norton explained to the class. "And I'm here to talk with you about sex. Anything you want to know, you can ask me. Now what do you want to know?" *I have never seen the phrases "sex" and "nurse" form a less arousing sentence than that one.*

I looked around the room at a mass of early teens who, not surprisingly, weren't leaping out of their seats to express their ignorance about fornication in front of their peers.

"You can ask whatever you want," she announced, as she passed out slips of paper. "Write down your questions, and put them in this box. Then I'll read them out loud anonymously and answer them. If you want to know where to get condoms, I can tell you that. If you want to know where to get *free* condoms, I can tell you that."

Wait, free condoms? I sat up in my chair. *Someone ask that question. And ask if adults can go there, too.*

"Are condoms expensive?" one of the students asked.

"Yeah," interjected one of the teachers as though she couldn't stop the words from coming out. We all gave a commiserating nod which probably didn't belong in this conversation.

"Or maybe," the sex nurse continued, "you want to know what percentage of high schoolers have had intercourse. It's not as many as you think." *Ooh, fun. Ask that, too. I want to know.* "Here, I'll tell you," she said. "Does anyone have a guess?"

Growing up, this question always made me feel insecure. It was my estimate that maybe 40 percent of our student body had done the deed, and it was also my estimate that I had definitely not. Where was this woman then, coming to tell me that it wasn't as bad as I thought? "Does anyone have any guesses?" she asked.

"Ninety-nine percent," said one smart ass.

"Two percent," said another.

"The truth is," she went on, "only 55 to 60 percent of them have had intercourse." *Wait, what? That's your can-you-believe-how-small-it-is-number? Are you freaking kidding me?! You just told 20 middle schoolers that if they don't screw anyone in the next four years, they're in the minority! I didn't even think 55 to 60 percent of adults were doing it.*

The teacher started going through the box. I was hooked. The first slip asked how old you should be to go on your first date, which she sidestepped brilliantly. The next read, "Why do guys always talk about their penises?" which was a fantastic question. The other male teacher had to tell them that, sadly, this did not change as you got older.

"Is that true, Mr. Krieger?" the sex nurse asked as she turned to me.

Huh? Why are you asking me? How is this the first time you're deciding to involve me in the conversation?

"Yes," I answered. Everyone laughed. Then I went back to being silent. I was elated to know that this was the entirety of my co-teaching responsibilities.

"Ooh, here's one," she said. "Why is it called getting your cherry popped?" Another great question for which I myself was curious to hear a response.

As the children laughed uncomfortably, the teacher drew a diagram of the vagina that even as an adult I didn't really understand and explained how when you penetrate the vagina for the first time, it breaks the hymen. *Sure, yeah, go on.* "So, a lot of people call that the cherry. And that's what gets popped," she explained. *Wait, so why is the hymen called the cherry?*

The class nodded as though she had effectively answered the question. *Wait, how was that a satisfactory explanation? Why is the hymen called the cherry??!!*

"Next question!" she announced. Then the bell rang. It was devastating.

The day continued onwards, and eventually it was 2:15 p.m. and time to go home. It had been nothing like what I expected. Everyone was relatively well-behaved, and I walked away with no signs of PTSD. The group dialogue was kind of fun, I had gotten a lot of work done on the blog while those videos were playing, and $70 wasn't nothing.

I guess getting my substitute-teaching cherry popped wasn't too painful after all. I only wish I knew why they called it that.

Odd Job #24: Writer/Entertainer

How I found the gig: Writing this blog
Time worked: Varies
Pay: Enough

Present Day (2015)

I am sitting in a local card room in New Hampshire. The tournaments here get a little under 100 participants, and the buy-ins run anywhere from $80 to $150, meaning first place usually wins somewhere around $2,000. I come up once every few months because I still enjoy the game, even if it's not the focus of my life that it once was.

My opponent, a 20-something kid I have faced a dozen times, made his bones playing poker online. He's never confirmed that, but I just know. Internet players are constantly betting, whether they have good cards or bad. It's an effective strategy that can fluster those around you, but it's also an easy way to sink yourself if you're not careful. You need what he has: a constant awareness of who's so afraid of you that they'll fold no matter what and who's so sick of your aggression that they'll call with anything.

But there's something else that makes him good: He plays without ego. Most guys his age try too hard to prove themselves when they face other talented players, making crazy bluffs and crazier calls. But the smart ones know you make your money picking on the weaklings. There's a line in the film *Rounders* where Matt Damon, talking about the professionals at a poker table, says, "We're not playing together. But then again, we're not playing against each other either. It's like the Nature Channel. You don't see piranhas eating each other, do you?" And that about sums it up.

So when this particular player is up against someone else who's good, he doesn't make fancy plays, he simply bets when he has it and folds when he doesn't. This all matters because he and I are the only ones still in the hand, and he's just made a big bet. If he thinks I'm among the elite then I can be quite sure I'm beat. But if he thinks I'm bad then he could easily have nothing.

I only have one problem: I stopped being elite a couple of years ago, and I don't know if he's figured that out yet.

Poker is a Darwinian game. The worst players either run out of money or get so tired of losing that they stop showing up, save for the few of them who get better. In turn, everyone else must either keep improving or wind up as the new weakest competitors in the room.

My time spent playing has dropped off dramatically, and the energy I once put into getting better at cards now goes into writing. It's a tradeoff I feel good about, except in these moments, when I'm facing a big bet and unsure what to do.

I look into his eyes, searching for a tell. A clue about what he has. He stares back at me, revealing nothing. I shuffle my chips, and I make calculations. But they lead me nowhere. If I call here, it wouldn't be because I think I have the better hand, it would be because I am hoping I do. And any time you're hoping in poker, you're in trouble.

"Fold," I mutter, and I toss my cards away. The most pathetic play in the game. Not one of those I've-read-my-opponent-perfectly-and-know-his-cards-are-better-than-mine kind of folds. There's pride in folds like that. Instead it's one of those I-have-no-idea-what-you-have-but-that's-a-lot-of-money-so-I-give-up folds. A surrender.

He doesn't show his cards. Good players rarely do. Instead he scoops the pot into his chip stack and gets ready for the next hand.

I don't lose to everyone now, but I lose more often than I used to. I'm like the past-his-prime pitcher who's still good enough to get some strikeouts and win some games, but whose fastball doesn't pop the catcher's mitt quite as hard as it used to and whose curveball has lost some of its break. I'm still decent, but decent isn't good enough.

You might assume that over the course of a night, roughly half the people in a poker room will win and roughly half will lose, but that's not the case. When you play, the house takes a portion of what you buy in for. It's called the rake, and it's how they make money. The rake often seems like a small amount when it comes out, but over the course of the night, across everyone there, it adds up to something huge. And whenever players win anything, they're expected to tip the dealer. These two deductions are enough to ensure that about 90 percent of the people in the room will lose money and five to seven percent more will finish around break-even. To turn a profit, you need to be among the top three percent of the field. And to make a living, you need to be even better.

And so the game has become for me what it is for most: gambling. An inevitable parting between me and my money.

Casinos are coming to my home state. Legislation to legalize online poker has been debated at the local and national level. As the former pro, and the person who used to send out those annoying please-contact-your-elected-officials e-mails urging people to join me in the fight to decriminalize internet gambling, friends ask me for updates and opinions about what's going on. But I have no answers. I shrug and say, "Ya know, I should be following that, but I'm not."

It's a bit disappointing to realize that the decline in playing time has softened my edge, but it's not a decision I regret. Poker is like the ex-girlfriend you care about but not "the one that got away." It's the one that you miss but that you now know was never right for you in the first place.

The *Odd Jobs* blog has given me a better path.

My routine of constantly picking up new gigs, then keeping the ones I enjoyed and dropping the ones I didn't, means that my laundry list of jobs has finally transitioned from a collection of poor-paying time sucks to an array of fun, ever-changing activities. I now love going to work every day.

In addition, the blog taught me how to not spend everything I earn. As a result, I have an income I can live on and enough money for savings, paying down debt, and enjoying life.

All the while, I have plenty of time left for writing. Which now, thanks to my blog, has become the part of my daily life I always wanted it to be.

Not to mention, the whole process is helping me create my first book. Something I've dreamed about since high school.

Sure it gets a bit difficult when I meet someone at a party and they ask me what I do. I'm still trying to figure out a one-word answer, but for now writer/entertainer is the closest I can get. I can tell that for some, my situation is so scattered they assume I must be lost. But for the first time in a long time I don't care what they think. I know I'm heading down a path that makes me happy, and I'm excited about where I'm going.

Several years ago, I sat in my living room and only half-listened as my father told me that someday I would view Black Friday, the day that online poker died, as one of the best things that ever happened to me. As he talked about turning lemons into lemonade.

Now I'm sitting at my desk, typing the final words of this book, looking back on how my life has changed. Looking forward to what's coming next.

And, though I always hate to admit it, it looks like my father did know what the hell he was talking about. But this time it doesn't taste like eating crow.

It tastes like lemonade.

WHERE DO I GET MORE?

Curious to read more of my work? Visit www.jonathankrieger.com. There you will find pieces from the past few years that I posted while working on my book, as well as some of the writings I've mentioned in the last couple hundred pages, like my interview with Peter Sagal or my thoughts after the bombings at the Boston Marathon. And now that I've concluded this project, I'll be posting new content a whole lot more often.

What am I going to write about? I'm not sure. But I'm excited to find out.

ACKNOWLEDGEMENTS

As I wrapped up college, I told my parents the exciting news: I would be putting almost none of my $150,000 education to use and was instead going to LA to become an actor, a career path that offered a miniscule chance of success and zero job security. They told me they loved me and supported me. When I told them I wanted to be a professional poker player, a career path that offered a miniscule chance of success and zero job security, they told me they loved me and supported me. And as I spent several years focusing on some silly blog that I hoped would become a book and kick off my life as a professional author—a career path that, that's right, offered a miniscule chance of success and zero job security—they told me they loved me and supported me.

Pursuing the fun path isn't always fun. There are times that are hard and dark and sad. And at some point you risk running out of the resolve you need to keep going. But resolve seems to last longer when people with big hearts are standing in your corner. Throughout my life, that has always been my parents.

Oh, and for those of you who read the back cover, I should clarify something: My father does know what an e-book is, he just let me use that quote because he thought it was funny. So he's a good sport, too.[61]

Speaking of unwavering support and love, there's my sister, who is a professional editor by day and volunteered her talents for this project. As I type these words, she is sitting across from me, poring over the latest draft of my book with her trademark red pen. It is probably the seventh time she has gone through the thing in its entirety.

The first time was a couple of years ago. I had been working on turning my blog into a book for about a year, and I was telling everyone how great it felt to almost be done. But the book wasn't there yet. She knew it, and on some level I did, too. My sister loved me enough to tell me I could do better, just as Ms. Middleton had years before.

I didn't want to hear it. What she was describing would require taking out entire sections, putting in new ones, and rewriting half the things in between. Even more upsetting, she was right. And man is it annoying when she's right. But, she told me, there was good news. Yes, I still had a long distance to go, but she would be right beside me the whole way.

Along with my parents and my sister, I also got great feedback from John Hargrave, Lily Mooney, and Pete Sestina, and I owe them all a big thanks for helping me make *Odd Jobs* the book that it is.

Thank you to Aleksandra Dabic for designing the cover, which I absolutely love. When Aleksandra submitted her first mock-up, I proposed about a dozen tweaks and changes. She painstakingly executed all of them, only for me to realize her original version was pretty much perfect. If you ever need a cover

---

[61] Having said that, my mother really does think this is the most brilliant book she's ever read.

for your book, check out her company, Mad Studio Designs,[62] even if you don't want a roll of toilet paper staring your readers in the face.

Thank you to Kate LaRue, who spent hours talking on the phone and putting prototypes together on her computer to educate me about what goes into a good cover. She helped me conceptualize and describe things I didn't even realize I was looking for. Thank you also to my cover advisers, including Mike Manship, Steven Johnson, Yael Langer, and many of the others mentioned in this section.

Thank you to Jacqueline Gallagher and Nathan Hepp, who helped construct the website I used to host the *Odd Jobs* blog. Thank you to the many friends who let me crash at their homes when I was between apartments and couch surfing. They include Andie Rizzolo, Bruce Vencil, Dave Hourihan, Greg Halloran, Jared Egan, Katty Halloran, Kerry Mullin, Michelle Slade, and several more referenced elsewhere in these acknowledgements. Thank you to Alea Mehler, Bruce Mehler, Colleen Carney, Charlotte Dore, Deric Bender, Ilana Marcus, Jared Kilgore, Lianne O'Shea, Rich Reninsland, and Sean Caron, all friends who helped me get gigs I wrote about on my site. And thank you to Michelle Falanga, who played my better half the time I was a conjoined twin.

Thank you to everyone who was a part of the Kickstarter process: the donors who backed the project, Adam Finelli for providing lights and his acting talent for the video campaign, and Evan Mehler, who both filmed the project and demonstrated amazing restraint by not strangling me every time I failed to hit my mark. Thank you to Margaret Willison for hosting the author

---

[62] https://www.facebook.com/madstudiodesigns/

Q&A at this book's launch party. Due to the constraints of the space-time continuum, I am forced to type these words before the event. But I'm sure that by the time you are reading this, she will have been fantastic.

Thank you to Emily Duggan, who took care of so many of the other things I needed done so I could focus on getting this damn thing out the door. Without her assistance, I might still be working on it.

Thank you to Bob Carney, David Goldstein, John Hargrave (again), Kookie Toro, Lorinda Falco, Melissa Ehlers, Paula Sullivan, Sam Jordan, and Shannon Lane DuPont. They gave me the jobs I actually held onto, the ones that ultimately allowed me to support myself doing work I loved while I wrote. When we think of the jobs we want, we concentrate on what we'd like to do. But one of the biggest factors impacting workplace happiness is how you feel about the person you answer to. Everyone I listed was more than just a boss. They were mentors, cheerleaders, and friends.

Thank you to all the great people in my life who believed in me. Who encouraged me as I wrote this blog. Who didn't roll their eyes when I said, "I think I'll be done with the book in a few months" for several straight years. They were cool about it when I said, "I'm sorry, I can't hang out, I have to dress up as Mickey Mouse and march in a parade." And, most important, they put their arms around my shoulders when I asked, "What the hell am I doing? Is anyone ever going to read this?"

Thank you to David Goodrich and Michael Stirk, who made me the nicest dessert I have ever seen when it was finally time to celebrate: a picture of my book on a cake.

Thank you to Scout Poulten for keeping me company as I

slaved away on *Odd Jobs* at the Wellesley public library while she worked on her own book. And, come to think of it, thanks to the patrons of the Wellesley public library for not shushing us every time we broke the strict "no talking" policy. And definitely thank you to the staffers who looked the other way as I broke the "no food" restriction with those essential-to-my-process M&Ms. Except for that one who came over and said, in the snarkiest tone imaginable, "Oh, I'm sorry, you must have missed the sign that said, 'No food allowed.'" You know who you are.

Thank you to Beverly Luskin, my first-grade teacher, who introduced me to the amazing world of writing. Thank you to Inez Middleton, who gave me all the support an English teacher ever could. And thank you to George Saunders, my college professor, who always provided the perfect feedback. I'm not sure if they remember me, but I'll never forget them.

And finally, thank you to you, the reader. When you exchanged your hard-earned money for this, my first-ever book, you made me think that maybe it's not totally crazy to believe that I could be a professional author.

Made in the USA
Middletown, DE
22 November 2018